never alone

THE DAY
I REALIZED I WAS DYING,
I REALLY BEGAN TO LIVE

TERRY SCHWARTZ

Pacific Press® Publishing Association
Nampa, Idaho
Oshawa, Ontario, Canada
www.pacificpress.com

Hart Research Center

Terry Schwartz enjoys taking photographs—portraits, almost—of animals. For the enjoyment of the readers of this book, Pacific Press® has reproduced a number of these photos in it. Terry has provided them and assumes full responsibility for them.

Cover design by Ani Holdsworth (Ani Designs)
Cover photo by Terry Schwartz
Back cover photo by David Lopez
Photos on pages 148 and 181 by Dina Schwartz
Photo on page 155 by Ron Priest
Inside design by Kristin Hansen-Mellish

The author assumes full responsibility for the accuracy of all facts and quotations as cited in this book.

You can obtain additional copies of this book by calling toll-free 1-800-765-6955 or by visiting http://www.adventistbookcenter.com.

ISBN 13: 978-0-8163-4114-6
ISBN 10: 0-8163-4114-1

12 13 14 15 16 • 5 4 3 2 1

To

Dina, Sheree, Terra, and my family:

I am planning on spending eternity with all of you.

Dina, you have always encouraged me to follow my dreams,

from photography to racing cars to traveling to Africa—even to Timbuktu!

Thank you for challenging me to be the best that I can be

and for encouraging me to pursue my passions.

For this and many other things,

I am forever grateful.

Contents

TOMORROW

Foreword

By JOHN ADAMS

In 2007, I awoke to the fact that was I spiritually empty. That realization led to some very honest conversations with God and eventually I began to pray for someone to come into my life who could mentor me by his example, advice, and inspiration. Of course, we have no idea how God will respond to that kind of prayer; we must simply wait and watch for the opportunities He provides us.

I was a divorced father, and I had also begun to search for opportunities to reconnect with my children. My eldest daughter, Alex, had participated in the Kansas-Nebraska youth mission trip the year before, and since I had grown up as a Seventh-day Adventist, I jumped at the chance to go on another mission trip that I hoped would give me the opportunity to reconnect with Alex. Little did I know the lasting effect this trip would have on me and what I would learn about God's plans for my future.

In the faraway land to which we went, I crossed paths with Terry Schwartz. I'd heard of him before this trip, but I knew very little about him. My first impression of him was that he must work in the construction trade as he had sun-leathered skin, large hands, and crooked fingers, which evinced numerous injuries. I thought his hands were an inkling of what Christ's hands might have looked like.

As the mission trip progressed, I observed Terry leading, guiding, nurturing, nudging, educating, encouraging, and at times barking at thirty-some adolescents and adults who were novices at construction as we tried to build a high-quality building. Every five or ten seconds you could hear someone yelling, "Terry!"—trying to get his attention. He responded each time, always taking the time to listen, always patient, always guiding as the project grew closer to completion. And amid all the demands made upon him and the encouragement he continually gave us, he took the time to grab his camera and take picture after picture and to put his arm around the various members of his crew just to tell them how important and helpful they were and what a great job they were doing. We all knew that Terry loved each of us individually.

In the time we spent together while traveling, building, and catching what rest we could in our tawdry hotel, Terry and I discovered threads of common experiences that tied us together. We became brothers. This mission trip opened the way to many deep conversations about life and its struggles and pain; about high school principals whom we had hated; and about new adventures in forgiveness and love. Because of what he has shown me of the love of God and because of his modeling love and acceptance of all people even while suffering the greatest of life's trials, I have been able to forgive and to release long-held hurts and pain.

During the past five years, we have traveled to Africa several times, spent long bus rides together, and talked late into the night in far-off lands. Terry always welcomes me into his home, invites me to go fishing with him, and leaves me in the snow-dust when we go skiing—all the while teaching this mindless photographer what he knows about bringing out the color and light of the scenes we shoot.

Since I have been with Terry in a wide variety of settings, I've had the opportunity to interact with many people from all over the earth who want to reconnect with their "good friend Terry." I watched him reach out in love to Kenneth, one of the poorest, filthiest men I have ever seen. I watched as Terry sat by the side of this lost man, put his arm around him, and loved him. *Loved* him!

As I saw this interaction, I couldn't help but believe that through Terry I was seeing how Christ embraced the poorest of the poor, the sickest of the sick, the most broken of the injured, and *loved* them. I felt that I had been like Kenneth when I first crossed Terry's path. I, too, was lost, hopeless, poor, and spiritually and emotionally empty. Terry's unselfish love and open arms redirected me and made me want to be a better man. His influence brought me to conversion and helped me choose to serve the Lord. He encouraged me to stand taller and to live a life of color, depth, and active investment of myself to meeting the needs of others.

Watching Terry care for Kenneth, I finally understood the meaning of God's grace and love. My brother Terry was a living, walking Bible story right in front of my eyes. I saw God's unselfish love in him, who, though he had both feet on death's doorstep and was living only by God's grace, loved and cared for all whom he met.

I am blessed to know Terry. He's been the mentor I prayed for. Oh, it's true that he's blemished. He hasn't lived a perfect life. But that's OK. In fact, that's what makes God's grace and love so evident in his life.

My brother Terry is the most generous, energetic, and loving man I know. Through him I have learned that God's love can forgive and transform someone like me.

One evening I asked Terry how he gets out of bed and faces life when he knows he's nearing death's door. He gave me a simple answer—one that I ask God every day for the strength and focus to follow. He looked me in the eye and said, "I pray constantly, all day long."

THE NINETY-DAY VERDICT

I have cancer, but cancer doesn't have me!

"*You have cancer. . . .*
"*Unfortunately, the Gleason score of your biopsy is a nine, the worst possible score. You have less than a one percent chance of being alive in ninety days.*"

CHAPTER 1

God's Plans

"Sometimes in the winds of change we find our true direction."

—Unknown

I sometimes wonder whether it's really possible that there is a Divine Being out there somewhere who is actually interested in me personally. If He owns everything, can make anything He wants, and can do anything He desires, why would I be of value to Him?

Does He really love me? Can I really love Him?

When I think about those questions, I am reminded of the times He has saved me from disaster—especially the times I thought I had "lucked out," or managed to squeak through by the skin of my teeth. I'm sure there are many more of those times than I can remember. *He really does love me!*

That's amazing, but even more amazing is the fact that this Divine Being designed me to follow a very specific life plan and then gave me permission to choose whether or not to follow it. I've spent much of my life pondering how I could discover and follow the life plan God has designed for me. What does He want me to be, and how can I get there? I once believed He wanted me to be doctor, but I disappointed myself and didn't reach that goal. If I can't reach my own hopes and goals, how can I possibly do what God expects of me?

My breakthrough moment came when I realized that *I was exactly where He wanted me to be*. Even though I had stumbled through many detours, I was on the track and headed toward God.

I was serving as construction superintendent for a Maranatha school-building project in Maputo, Mozambique. Pastor Dick was the spiritual leader for the trip, and he had chosen Jeremiah 29:11 as the theme for the devotionals: "God has a plan for my life, a plan for good things and not bad, a plan for a future filled with hope" (paraphrased). That week I chose to really take personal ownership of that verse and let God lead.

Finally, my past made perfect sense to me. God hadn't wanted me to be a doctor. He wanted me to be a carpenter! Every wilderness experience, every dead end, and every misstep had equipped me uniquely to be me. He's not finished with me yet! I'm not perfect by any means, but I am willing to be called and shaped.

Have you ever started a project—perhaps building a replica of the *Titanic,* renovating a room in your house, or some other project that seems to have no end, and when you finally do see the end, it isn't what you had signed up for? Sometimes I imagine that's how God feels about us, His carefully created earthly family. The biggest difference is that we are *exactly* what God signed up for. He knows what's coming. He has counted the cost. He always finishes what He starts. Yes, it seems to take forever, and we take Him on the hardest roads with the most detours. Fortunately, God is patient. He never gives up on us even if we do. I'm thankful that He's never given up on me!

Many times each day I ask God to control my life, to straighten my path, to help me meet the constant challenges the devil plants in the path. There are many areas of my life that still need work, and as my Master Sculptor, God is chiseling, sanding, and shaping me, creating a personalized masterpiece. His eye is always on me. His touch is constant, unchanging, and sure. Most amazing of all, He is transforming me into His image!

God, I'm humbled by that thought. Thank You for not giving up on me.

Each of us exists for a reason. God didn't allow you or me to be born because earth needed another human. Our planet is already home to more than seven billion people! Quantity isn't the issue. Purpose is. You and I exist because our heavenly Father wants us to exist. We are His unique creation. He's given us a mix of talents and capabilities unlike that of any other person. And along with those gifts, He's given us a purpose that no other person can fulfill.

God, thank You for making each of us special—and for guiding each of us individually to the place where we can serve You best.

It's impossible to find silver that's 100 percent pure, even in a silver mine. You find silver mixed together with a number of other elements. To get the 99 percent pure silver that's used in U.S. Silver Eagle coins, the coin maker has to put the ore through a refining process that burns away all the dross. When you put silver in a fire to refine it, you have to keep it there just the right amount of time. If you leave it there too long, the fire will burn it up. If you take it out too soon, it will still be full of impurities. That's a pretty good metaphor for what God is doing in my life.

Unfortunately, it's taken some pretty hot fires to refine me! Every now and again, God has to throw a few more logs on the fire to reheat me. The fire He uses to refine me is unique to me—a combination of challenges and opportunities that fit my personality perfectly and that are slowly bringing out His character in me. He's doing the same thing with you: providing personalized purification!

There have been times when I rebelled at the fire and tried to put it out. I thought I could grow and improve on my own—that I didn't need His help. That doesn't work. I've learned that if I am going to come out of the fire stronger, less blemished, and with a character more like that of my Creator, I have to trust Him to do His work His way.

Personal growth is a journey on a path that stretches as far ahead of us as our lives do.

John Lennon said, "Life happens while you're busy making other plans." I was one of those people who spent their lives making the plan, working the plan, believing they're on course and in control—just to have the perfect storm take me in an entirely different direction and throw me up on the rocks when I got there.

I hadn't included cancer in my life plan, but when the doctors told me I had cancer and that the disease had left me with only ninety more days of life, I decided to embrace the disease as part of God's plan. If this is OK with Him, it doesn't necessarily mean that I'm going to die tomorrow; it means that He's going to use my cancer as a refiner's fire. It will be hot, but helpful.

Hearing the cancer diagnosis was one of the strangest things I've ever experienced. The doctors told me to go home and get my things in order because I was going to die. I refused to believe them. I had family, employees, tenants, and friends counting on me to continue to do all the things I had always done for them. I didn't have time for this. Yet somewhere in the furthermost recesses of my mind, a clock started counting off the days toward the total they said I had left.

Almost immediately, establishing priorities became important to me. Those priorities were different from the ones I'd had before the prognosis. Suddenly, some things I had thought were very important lost their importance, and other things that hadn't been on my radar now took first place in life. I immediately realized that some things I hadn't given enough time to must now become the most important things in life. My priorities now shifted to spending time with my girls, my wife, my parents, my siblings, and my friends. Relationships—meaningful ones—took first place!

My cancer refocused me on the one priority that will never change for me. I am here to serve God. Every other priority revolves around Him—the One who gives me stability and purpose.

People are the real joy of life; everything else is just stuff that is overrated. We are a lot like snowflakes, both in uniqueness and fragility. No two of us are completely alike, even if we've come out of the same cloud or shared the same storm. I have chosen to let each of my loved ones know that I love them today and will continue to love them tomorrow. I've committed myself to hugging them every chance I get. There's a limit on how long I'm going to be able to do that. That limit is called life, and I want to be sure I give and receive all of the love possible while I'm here.

The day I was diagnosed with cancer I also committed myself to living the rest of my life doing only the things I was passionate about. That really shifted and narrowed my focus. A lot of stuff just went away, crowded out by the important.

Standing on the gas pedal of my old Camaro and accelerating to 165 miles an hour in nine seconds was no longer as important to me as hugging my girls. Except for family, very few things matched the value of building a school in Africa or meeting the needs of broken people.

Suddenly, it didn't matter if I had ninety days or ninety years. I resolved to spend all of the time I had left doing what God impressed me to do. That decision made my inner self happier than it had been in a long time! The moment I realized I was dying became bittersweet, because it was also the moment when I really began living.

The truth is, we're all dying—we just don't think about it. None of us has an expiration tag where we can read it. It's weird that I had to hear someone saying "ninety days" before I allowed God to refocus my priorities.

We're all navigating uncharted waters. Many of us don't check the compass as often as we should; we sail on by the seat of our pants—until the big storm hits. It's when our boat begins to capsize that we wake up to reality, check the charts, change course, and make some choices we hope will keep us alive. Maintaining course when the weather was good didn't seem so important. As long as we had those conditions, we knew that we could get back on track with some small course corrections. Now the storm was forever altering my course, and I had no choice but to ride it out.

Crucial events change our lives. An auto accident, a ninety-day pronouncement, a heart attack, or a hastily spoken word. Each of these is a life changer, a moment that demands change. Very few of us embrace change. We don't have time for it, and we think we don't need it. The reality is that change is the one constant in life. Sometimes it comes in big waves that cause destruction on the level of a tsunami. Sometimes it comes in little ripples like those made by a small pebble in a big pond. Regardless, we have to live with each change. We do that best when we accept it, consider God's guidance, and move forward.

I'll never forget selling our first business. Dina was nervous, wondering how we would support ourselves. Our daughters were more certain about the decision. "Dad," they said, "we have never worried about you, and we're not going to start now." I was taking a dive into the unknown; trading a sure thing for something behind "door number 2." That was the first of three career changes I've made; each one voluntary, challenging, scary, and rewarding. Each one a headfirst dive into the fearful unknown. Each one a new turn in God's plan for me.

The ninety-day pronouncement was far worse than any of the changes or storms I had experienced up to that time. I was going to be facing some major changes. Embracing change and exploring the unknown with gusto is usually for the Marco Polo types. The rest of us, like me, prefer to be in complete control of our lives, to have few surprises—and no bad ones. We so easily overlook the fact that change provides new opportunities for personal growth. We tend to be so focused on treading water that we forget to learn new strokes.

Every storm takes us out of our comfort zones—which gives us the opportunity to do a personal makeover. And often, the tougher the storm, the more intense our scrutiny as to where we are and where we really should be. When the doctors told me I had cancer, I had to dig down really deep to find the courage to see the storm as an opportunity, an invitation. When they gave me ninety days, I had to dig even deeper. I didn't want this and would have loved to run from it, but that wasn't possible. However, as I dug deep, I found that God was waiting to help me. He eagerly offered me courage as I reached out in desperation.

My life has become a complicated mix of doctors, research, mission trips, family time, and much more. When the doctors began talking about short times and impossibilities, I decided that if these were somehow a part of God's plan, then I had better make the best of it. We are each given about fifteen hundred minutes every day, so I sat down with Dina, my wife, to determine how we could best use ours.

Has it been an easy walk? No. Life is not for sissies. But the personal growth I have experienced by facing my life challenges head-on has been tremendous. God still has plans for me, only His plans are far better than anything I could come up with on my own.

Somehow in the winds of change, I found my true direction. My life would never be the same. In many ways, it would be better.

Answered Prayer

I asked for strength that I might achieve;
    I was given weakness that I might obey.
I asked for health that I might do greater things;
    I was given grace that I might do better things.
I asked for riches that I might be happy;
    I was given poverty that I might be wise.
I asked for power that I might have the praise of men;
    I was given weakness that I might feel the need for God.
I asked for all these things that I might enjoy life;
    I was given life that I might enjoy all things.
I received nothing that I asked for, but all that I hoped for.
    My prayer was answered.

CHAPTER 2

A Broken Wing

Dear God,
Thank You for extending the days of my life so You could complete Your purpose in me. Please continue to shower me with the grace to serve You more wholeheartedly.

This part of my story really begins in Mozambique. I was building a school there with a group of Maranatha volunteers. We were in Beira, a coastal town that is extremely hot and humid. The building was huge, designed to hold more than four hundred students. The local Maranatha workers had already assembled the steel framework, so our job was to build concrete block walls on the exterior of the building and as the interior walls between the classrooms. Some of these walls were to be more than twenty feet high.

While climbing down from a high scaffold, I foolishly chose to take a shortcut and jumped the remaining five feet to the ground. Unfortunately, my left foot landed on a stone. It hurt, but I can live with pain. So, thinking that it was just bruised and would heal on its own, I continued working—though limping as I did so—for the remainder of our time in Mozambique. After all, there was still work to be done!

When we finally got back to Lincoln, Nebraska, where I live, I had our family doctor do a quick X-ray. He told me that a bone in my foot had been broken, but that it looked like I had taken good care of it and that it should heal pretty soon. I was glad that I didn't have to have any more procedures done on my foot because we had scheduled a trip to Thailand and Cambodia with our daughters Terra and Sheree, and I didn't want anything to slow me down or keep me from traveling to one of my favorite places with my favorite girls.

Terra and Sheree had planned our itinerary. We walked through most of Bangkok. I had bought a special shoe that kept my foot stable while also giving the bone room to heal. So I kept right on walking through Thailand and Cambodia wearing out three of those "healing shoes" as we toured.

We took a train to the mountain city of Chang Mai, where we photographed tigers and orchids. We rode elephants, and we watched artisans carve intricate designs into furniture panels. My daughters had done an excellent job of placing me where my cameras would be busy!

In Cambodia, we spent several days at the temples of Angkor Wat. I love that place! Even though I am fascinated by the skill of the Incas and would travel with you to Machu Picchu in a minute, the amazing stone city there is only postage-stamp size in comparison with the temples of Angkor Wat. I added ten thousand more "faces and temple" photos to my files during the time we spent there.

Our first trip to the temple site, though, was more than a little unnerving. When we arrived at the hotel near the place, I asked the man at the desk how we could get to the temples in time for a perfect sunrise photograph.

"One of my friends has a *tuk-tuk*," he said. "To get to the temple for sunrise, you must leave here at three thirty in the morning. He'll be here to pick you up."

We agreed to the appointment, but we went to bed assuming we'd never see the *tuk-tuk* man.

The next morning, the alarm rang at 3:00 A.M. I looked out the window, and surprise of surprises, the *tuk-tuk* driver was waiting in front of the hotel and smiling! We dressed, grabbed our cameras and backpacks, and dashed downstairs.

A *tuk-tuk* is a motorized tricycle with a board seat over the back wheels. Most have a bright orange canopy over the passengers, providing them a bit of shelter from the intense sun and enough protection during the monsoon rains to keep your hat dry. This *tuk-tuk* had room for three individuals, or a family of four.

Our driver, Tony, was a young teenager who didn't speak a word of English, and we knew no Khmer. "Angkor Wat temple," I said.

After a few minutes of bad sign language, he understood where we wanted to go and roared off into the early morning. Ten minutes later, we came to a divide in the road. A sign there bore the word *Temple* and pointed north. But our driver turned west on a small lane that quickly became a terrifying dark alley. I had this really bad feeling.

"Temple!" I yelled over the roar of the *tuk-tuk*.

Tony pointed straight ahead.

"But the sign said that way," I objected and pointed north.

"Temple," he said, pointing west and continuing to drive in the wrong direction.

It didn't look good, but we settled lightly back onto the seat, sure we were being kidnapped on our first morning in Cambodia.

Five minutes later, I abandoned my patience, grabbed our kidnapper tight enough to hurt him, and commanded that he return to the fork in the road and take us to the temple. He pried my arms loose and pointed straight ahead. "Temple!"

He was right. A few minutes later, we pulled up onto the main temple road,

having saved much time due to his shortcut. Dina and I were hugely relieved!

We hired Tony for the day. He charged thirteen U.S. dollars for the entire day. No doubt the twenty dollars I gave him was some of the best money I've ever spent. He took us wherever we wanted to go and waited—sometimes for two hours!—till we had taken our last picture, returning us to our hotel long after the sun had gone down. And the next morning, he was waiting for us again at 3:30 A.M.!

We spent four days at Angkor Wat, yet I never got the sunrise picture I had envisioned. The first day, we assumed that we would be the only people there, but when we arrived, a crowd of five hundred or more people was jostling for camera position! Then the clouds were in the wrong place, the wind was too strong, the light wasn't right, or something else made that special photo impossible.

Tony became a very good friend. We were probably some of the best-paying customers he had ever taken down that dark alley. At the end of our last full day in Cambodia, we settled our account and said our goodbyes to Tony in front of our hotel. We also exchanged addresses. I wanted to be sure I could have him as my driver again the next time I came to Cambodia because he was so good at getting us to our intended destinations. And besides, he had kidnapped our hearts!

As we were finishing our goodbyes, I stepped up to the *tuk-tuk* to give Tony a hug. When I stretched my arms toward him, my left leg leaned right into the motorcycle's exhaust pipe, and it instantly barbecued a four-by-six-inch section of my leg. But it was the end of the day, and I didn't want to go to a Cambodian emergency room, so we went back to our hotel room and broke out the aloe vera. The next morning we flew home to Nebraska.

Three days later, Maranatha had us on another airplane, this one heading for Temuco, Chile, with a group of adults from all parts of the United States. We were building a beautiful red-brick church right in front of a large Seventh-day Adventist school. I did my best to walk without limping, but the volunteers soon realized that I wasn't functioning at full strength, and they worked hard to care for me during the entire trip.

By now I was coating the burned patch on my leg every day with what seemed to be pints of aloe vera, and I had progressed to crutches because my foot was so painful. I probably should have flown straight home and gone to a doctor. Instead, Dina and I finished the Maranatha project we had been planning for months and then flew to southern Argentina for four days in the mountains. More walking, and more aloe vera.

When we finally got home, the doctor took one look at the hideous mass that had developed on my leg and told me that I would have to have major skin grafts. The next day the "mass" on my leg fell off. It was just a scab, and beneath it was pink new skin. I was healed, thanks to our persistence with aloe vera.

I know this sounds crazy, but two weeks later we were on yet another airplane, this time headed to Pucallpa, Peru, with another Maranatha group. We were on a project where the buildings were so filled with history that I wished the walls and floors could tell their stories. Our assignment was to renovate, remodel, paint, and tile the buildings at the original airbase from which Clyde Peters and other early Adventist aviators used to fly mission and rescue flights throughout the Amazon.

We really enjoyed our time at the base. We were working with a fantastic group of Kansas-Nebraska young adults. Together we got a lot of work accomplished and had a muddy but great time while doing it.

The heavy rains produced thick, sticky mud that was difficult to navigate through on crutches. After more than one slide in the mud, I was ready to go home and have my landing gear surgically repaired.

CHAPTER 3

"You Have Cancer"

"In the depth of winter, I finally learned that within me there lay an invincible summer."

—Albert Camus

I went first to our family doctor in Lincoln. He examined the foot and referred me to a very kind orthopedic surgeon who gave my pain a name. "You have a Jones fracture," he told me. "If your foot had broken a half-inch in any other direction, it would have healed already, but because it broke at exactly this location, it will never heal unless you have a nice shiny stainless-steel pin installed."

I was happy to have him fix it, but before he would begin, he asked me to get a physical to be sure that I was healthy enough for surgery and that there wasn't anything else that needed work while I was on his operating table. I've gotten a full physical every year, especially since my father had prostate cancer and my mother died of breast cancer. It was time for this year's physical, so I asked him to give me the whole deal. I was having to use the restroom more frequently, and I was having to get up more at night and had begun to fear—though I didn't say anything about it—that I might be coming to some cancer speed bumps. I wanted to catch it early if I was going to get it. I had no clue of what was coming.

The physical gave me clearance for the foot surgery, and the pin went in just fine. However, the next day I received a letter saying I had an appointment with a urologist. I hadn't scheduled any appointment with a urologist, so I called our family doctor's office and asked what was going on. I was told: "Your blood test showed that your PSA—a significant indicator for prostate cancer—is seventeen. That's exceptionally high, and it's also a very disturbing jump from last year's PSA of 1.22."

I went in for a biopsy, which involves the doctor taking some tissue samples from my prostate. All the while I was wondering why the Holy Spirit was dragging me home right now. Why was this happening to me this month? How could I work for God, be His servant, and be threatened by cancer all at the same time? I was worried, and I wasn't sure how I should be feeling.

The next morning, May 22, I awoke at my usual time of 5:15, showered, ate breakfast, and went out on the porch with Dina to watch the cardinals, orioles, and finches at our bird feeder. It was a cool, calm, wonderful Nebraska spring morning. Dina suggested that we slip into town and buy some pastries to surprise the women who worked for us at our daycare center. I agreed, and was putting my shoes on when the phone rang. It was Casey, a good friend of mine who was a physician's assistant at the urologist's office. I've known him since he was a little fellow. I wasn't at all prepared for what came next.

"Terry, I couldn't possibly have worse news for you," Casey said, his voice breaking a little. I braced for whatever he might say next. I could tell that he didn't want to tell me what he had to.

Then it came. "Terry," he said, "you have prostate cancer."

I glanced at my watch. It was 7:35 A.M., and my world had just turned upside down. I went from enjoying an absolutely beautiful morning to feeling as though I had been punched in the gut. I couldn't breathe, and I couldn't think about anything except my wife and daughters. I had been dreading a call like this for fifteen years, and now that it had come, I was struggling to know how to deal with it!

Several years earlier, my father's surgeon had pulled my brother Bruce and me aside after he had completed Dad's prostate surgery. "The probability that you both will have prostate cancer isn't 99 percent; it's 100 percent. That's how large a role genetics plays in this disease. You will have prostate cancer sometime." Ever since that day, I had prayed for science to find a cure for prostate cancer before it struck our family again.

Wrong prayer. I should have been praying for God to give me strength and courage and wisdom to face the disease when it arrived.

That certainly was what I was praying for now. Desperately.

Casey spoke again. "Unfortunately," he said, "the Gleason score of your biopsy is a nine, the worst possible score."

The Gleason score is a combination of two numbers, both on a scale of five. The first number indicates how much cancer is found, and the second number indicates the aggressiveness of the cancer. Men with prostate cancer usually don't live long enough to score a ten—the top or bottom of the chart, depending on how a person views it. I had scored a nine, which was reached in the worst possible way: a four plus a five. Four, almost the very worst score possible for the amount of cancer they found, plus five, which indicated that my cancer involved the very worst type of aggressive cancer cells.

"How serious is this?"

"Well, it's just a guess, but I think you have from three to six months."

Casey and I both paused to think through a few of the ramifications of his pronouncement. I immediately thought of Dina and the girls. He thought of his office schedule.

Even though there had always been a tiny prostate cancer worry at the back of my mind, I had never expected to experience this kind of an upside-down day. I had never planned on hearing someone tell me, "You have ninety days to live"—especially when I was feeling fine! I was cancer-shocked, and I chose to be God-directed. That took me to the Bible; specifically, to the book of Nehemiah.

Nehemiah was a talented Jewish captive who served as cupbearer to Xerxes the Great, king of Persia. Visitors to the Persian capital told Nehemiah that his city, Jerusalem, was lying waste—jackals were chasing rabbits through the ruins of its walls. That sent Nehemiah to his knees, and then to the king. When the king asked Nehemiah what was wrong, he took a deep breath, prayed to the Lord, and then said to the king—

Praying to God didn't require that I kneel and close my eyes. Nehemiah shows me that people can talk to God at the very moment when they are facing one of life's tough challenges. That was what I was doing as I held the phone and thought about Casey's tests—praying to God and speaking to Casey.

"I think I can get you in Monday morning for a few more tests." Casey said. "We'll do a full body scan to check for gross metastases."

That meant tumors in my language.

"Doc," I said, "is there any chance we can get started today?"

"OK," he answered. "Can you be here in ten minutes? You can drink the magic potion, and in a couple hours we can put you on the machine."

I was ready to go to work, but instead drove straight to his office to drink the juice.

Before I left the house, I did something that became a defining moment in this whole cancer adventure. As I stood in the bathroom to brush my teeth, worlds of worries, hopes, and fears overwhelmed me. I bowed my head and prayed a prayer I can remember—every word—more than three years later. "God, I am recommitting my life to You. I know that according to the doctors there is not much left of this body, but if You can still use me, I would still like to be used. But remember, I am here to do as You will." Then I took a deep breath and drove to the doctor's office. Praying and driving.

While driving, that little voice inside my head began to calm me and to re-focus my mind, and I thanked God for allowing me to break my foot in such a way that the doctors would find my cancer. I then asked for forgiveness for my hardheadedness, which kept me from caring for my foot six months earlier! My life focus had been sharpened—forever changed for the better. That's one of the gifts that cancer brought.

I've known many people who have had cancer, and it seems that everyone processes the news differently. The complete gamut of emotions floods over you, and no two people react in the same way. For some it is too painful to talk about. Others start a blog.

A fellow came to our church once and talked about what happens when you receive terrible, upsetting news—such as "You have only ninety days to live." He said that first you become angry at God. I never had that happen. I have never felt this was God's fault or something that should make me hate Him.

I was twelve when my mother died of breast cancer. I got really angry at God because He was taking my mother away. He let me down. He messed up my life without even asking my permission. He just took her! That made me *really* angry.

Yet now, when it's *my* life that's on the skids, I haven't felt that anger. Instead, I've been filled with concern for the people who depend on me. I certainly don't want my two beautiful daughters and my amazing wife to feel the way I felt when my mom died.

What will happen to Dina and our girls? What will happen to the employees at our daycare center? What about Dad and my siblings?

We're all going to die, but you don't want to say, "Well, I'm gonna be done in three months." But that thought was spinning through my head! *Wow, I'm supposed to be the provider for this household and for other households that depend on me. What is this going to do to them? I'm a great fixer, but how can I fix this?*

As I think back over to how I responded to the loss of my mom and how I responded to the sentence of death that I received, I see a significant difference between my twelve-year-old little-boy response, and my old man, husband, father, manager, owner response. When I was twelve, I only knew how to think about me, so my response was entirely self-centered. This time I've got a lot of people who depend on me, and I'm looking into their lives rather than my own. How will this affect them? That instantly became my greatest concern.

Anger at God? I didn't have time for that! My optimistic nature also kicked in. "Well, Doc, that may be what you and other medical people think will happen to me, but I'm not sure it *has* to be *that* way!"

I arrived at the clinic and drank the radioactive milkshake so they could do the scan later that day. A CT scan of my bones followed the next Tuesday. That gave the medical experts the data they needed to counsel me on the "next steps."

While they were working through the data, I dived into researching prostate cancer and all possible treatments for the disease. My days were a mix of online research, reading from half a dozen different books, and desperately praying for God to guide us in the direction He wanted us to go.

CHAPTER 4

Three Docs and a Fleece

"Not everything that is faced can be changed. But nothing can be changed until it is faced."

—James Arthur Baldwin

Several days after the bone scan and the other tests, we met with Dr. Howe, a local urologist. He was a pleasant man who exuded professionalism and care. He checked me thoroughly, explained the results of my tests, and scheduled me for prostate-removal surgery on the seventh of July. That was almost seven weeks away. I didn't want to wait—especially not for seven weeks!

Dr. Howe had good medical reasons for me to wait. If prostate surgery is done too soon after a biopsy, it can tear the intestine or damage it in other ways. Then I'd probably have to have a colostomy, and I knew I didn't want that. The biopsy had punched ten good-sized holes into the wall of my large intestine, and Dr. Howe said we needed to give them time to heal before having the surgery.

I understood all of that, but was still uncomfortable with the seven-week wait. I felt like I had a time bomb ticking inside me. If there was something inside me that was killing me, I wanted it out *today,* not two months from today.

We continued to pray for guidance, pleading with God to keep us heading down the right path. Not knowing for sure whether we were doing the right thing was by far the most difficult aspect of those days. Then I decided to ask God for my very first "fleece."

The Bible story about Gideon and his fleece offers an at times humorous picture of this common human desire. Gideon was a young Israelite who, in a dream, heard a voice speak to him. *"I want you to go out and lead the Israelite army against your enemies,"* the voice said.

"Yes, sir!" Gideon responded—and then he stayed up the rest of the night trying to figure out whether the voice he heard was God's, and what following the voice might mean for himself and his family.

By morning, Gideon wasn't sure if he'd heard God's voice or if he'd just eaten too much pizza for supper. Yet all day he was troubled by an intense pounding in his brain that said, *"God wants you to lead the Israelites against the Midianites."* So that evening Gideon took a woolen fleece, spread it out on the ground, and asked God for a sign, an indication of what God wanted him to do—which was just what I wanted too. Gideon prayed, "If it was really You who spoke to me, and if You really want me to lead an army against Midian, and if this war is really going to be a success, please make this fleece be soggy wet in the morning."

Gideon slept soundly that night, knowing that God would either make the fleece wet or keep it dry. Either way, he would *know* what God wanted him to do.

In the morning, the fleece was wet. Soaking wet! It *had been* God's voice, and Gideon *was* supposed to lead the army. I can imagine him running into the house with the soggy fleece in his hands and shouting, "God answered my prayer! Look, He made the fleece wet!"

That's when the family said, "God didn't make the fleece wet; the dew did!"

In Gideon's haste to get the right answer, he had made a dumb request. If you leave a nice fluffy lamb's wool fleece on the lawn overnight, it will be wet in the morning. Especially when the dew is heavy.

Humiliated, Gideon went back to God that evening. "God, I'm sorry. I blew it last night, so tonight I'm going to try to get the sign right, OK? If the voice I heard telling me to lead the Israelites against the Midianites really was Yours, and if this is going to be a successful war, please make the fleece *dry* in the morning." Then he set the fleece where the dew would be the heaviest and went to bed.

I doubt that Gideon slept much that night, and if he did, he dreamed of wet grass and a dry fleece.

According to the story, God was patient with Gideon and gave him a very dry fleece that next morning. And Gideon called up the army.

I remembered Gideon's story and dreamed of a fleece we could lay before God. Here's what we did. "God," we prayed, "You know what the docs are planning. You also know that it will be six weeks before they can do surgery. If You have a way to move the surgery closer to today, we'll follow Your lead."

Almost as soon as we prayed that prayer, we received an e-mail from Sheree, our eldest daughter. She was doing HIV research in South Africa. "Dad," she said, "you ought to check this out." Sheree was a doctoral student at Johns Hopkins University. The link she sent was to a Johns Hopkins outpatient center for cancer treatment.

I took a look at the link very late in the day. The Web site had a description of what Johns Hopkins does for prostate cancer, along with pictures of the doctors and a phone number. I dialed the number, and a very nice lady answered the phone, listened to my story, and told me that they were booking consultations for mid-August, twelve weeks away.

"My Gleason score is a nine, and I'm not sure I can wait that long," I told her.

"Please fax me your full pathology report," she said, "and I'll have a doctor look at it."

I faxed the papers immediately, praying as every page flew off to Baltimore.

About twenty minutes later, at 6:20 p.m. Baltimore time, a very nice doctor called me back. The conversation was very sobering.

"Mr. Schwartz, this is Dr. Han at Johns Hopkins University Medical Center. I have reviewed the lab reports that you have faxed us, and I must be very blunt with you. We have never cured anyone with your pathology. Based on the five hundred thousand people that share your Gleason score, we do not recommend surgery, as the cancer will not be contained. There is no point in putting you through the surgery as it is a very high risk operation that will not succeed. We will not be able to get all of the cancer. Your best option might be radiation. That might buy you a little more time."

I was devastated and silent. Then Dr. Han asked a very strange question. "Mr. Schwartz," he said, "how did you get the phone number you called earlier? It's an unlisted number."

I told him that I had been praying for the right doors to open, and that God had impressed me to call this number at the Johns Hopkins outpatient center.

"Mr. Schwartz, what church do you belong to?" Dr. Han asked.

"I am a Seventh-day Adventist Christian."

Dr. Han told me that he was also a Christian, but when I asked him what church he went to, he couldn't remember. "It has been too long," he said. Then he asked me my age, height, and weight.

"I am extremely busy and will be out of the office next week," he said. "I may or may not call you back. If you would like, you could FedEx your glass slides to our lab, and at least we can review them."

I hung up and immediately drove to the lab to retrieve the glass slides and made sure they were delivered to Dr. Han's office first thing the next morning.

My phone rang at eight fifteen the next morning. "Mr. Schwartz," said Dr. Han, "is there a chance that you could be in Baltimore in two days?"

"Yes," I told him.

"I cannot make any promises, but I would like to at least take a look at you."

I began searching for airline tickets. And that same day I called an oncologist friend named Mark—it's good to have friends!—and asked if I could see him. He was very accommodating, and at three o'clock that afternoon, Dina and I were sitting in his office. I explained my situation and told him about my conversation with Dr. Han. Mark was very pleasant and answered all of our questions. Then, as we were about to leave, Mark handed me a stack of papers. "I've researched your situation," he said, "and I suggest that you participate in one of the four clinical trials we have going right now. I have numbered these papers in the order I think might be the most valuable. Unfortunately, there won't be any benefit directly to you, but there might be benefit for future patients with prostate cancer. And Terry, I would encourage you to donate your body to science. That would be a great help in our ongoing studies."

We left Mark's office with a stack of papers and many prayers in our hearts. The next day we were Johns Hopkins bound, following our fleece.

Friday morning we set the alarm early to make sure that we would be on time for our consultation with Dr. Han. The outpatient center is served by a parking lot that must hold ten thousand cars. We circled and circled until finally another vehicle left and we were able to park where it had been, on level ten. This place was busy!

The building that houses the outpatient center is six floors tall and covers at least an entire city block. Walking in, I felt as though I were entering a huge shopping mall where hundreds of people were coming and going all of the time—rather like the Mall of America at Christmastime. But there was a big difference. All of the people looked like they had just returned from a war. They were walking with crutches or being pushed in wheelchairs, and most of them were wearing splints or casts. I felt almost out of place in my street clothes.

We exited the elevator on the fourth floor and found our way to Dr. Han's office. I stepped up to the receptionist and gave her my name. Her response dumbfounded me. "I am sorry, Mr. Schwartz," she said. "Are you sure you have the right day? Dr. Han doesn't come in on Fridays."

"That's really odd," I replied. "Dr. Han called me personally and set up this appointment."

That raised her eyebrows even higher. She turned to her computer, clicked away for a full minute, and then shook her head and looked up at me. "This is really strange," she said. "You *do* have an appointment today! Please take a seat as Dr. Han is in surgery and must be coming here just to see you."

About an hour later a tall, physically fit doctor strode into the waiting room still in full surgical scrubs. He walked right over to us, picking us out of the many others in the waiting room, put out his hand, and smiled. "Hello, Mr. Schwartz," he said. "I will be with you in a few minutes. Please come in."

We were then escorted to a small examination room. As I prepared for the exam, I thought about our fleece and said a short prayer. "God, please give this doctor even more wisdom than he would ever have on his own, and please give me the wisdom to know how to respond to what he says."

Shortly thereafter, Dr. Han stepped briskly into the room and sat down next to us. After a pleasant greeting, he got right down to business. "Mr. Schwartz, our lab has reviewed your pathology and unfortunately it is correct: your Gleason score is an inoperable nine. But I want to examine you anyway."

I was wearing a blue T-shirt with the words "Maranatha Volunteers" on it, along with a picture of a church, a cross, and "Chile" in big letters. Dr. Han asked about the shirt. I told him that we belonged to a volunteer organization that builds at least one church or school building somewhere in the world every day. I briefly shared that we had worked on buildings with Maranatha in Africa, Chile, and Peru in the last few months. "I had planned to go on a trip to Africa with my family, but it had to be canceled," he said.

He was clearly interested in our work with Maranatha and asked again what church we attended. Then, seeing I was using crutches, he wanted to know how I had hurt my foot. "You know, Dr. Han," I began to explain, "I am actually thankful that God allowed me to break my foot. Treating that foot was what led my doctors to discover the cancer." We talked about the trips, the buildings, the local people, and I mentioned that Maranatha trips usually have participants from many different church backgrounds.

"When my six-month-old son is a bit older, I will join you," Dr. Han said, and then he quickly switched back to business. Looking me straight in the eye, he said, "Mr. Schwartz, I will do your surgery, but God will have to do the rest. Without surgery, your life span would be measured in months, not years. I hope I'm not making a mistake. The type of cancer you have wouldn't even be slowed down by radiation. I will do your surgery."

"I feel like I have won the lottery!" I exclaimed. Then I remembered the fleece.

Looking down at me, Dr. Han said, "I can assure you, Mr. Schwartz, that you have *not* won the lottery. Let me check my schedule to see when we can fit you in."

I had brought a 465-page-long book with me: *The Official Guide to Surviving Prostate Cancer*. In the book I had found the Han Chart, a detailed description of prostate cancer intensity and the possibilities of survival. Unfortunately, I fit in the very last square on the chart—the square where everyone dies.

"Are you the author of this chart?" I asked.

"I am," he replied, "but it's really no big deal."

That was the first of many glimpses I have had of how special and humble this man is. As he left the room, I turned to Dina and said, "If God wants me to be here, we'll be back within two weeks. Remember the fleece!" As busy as they were at Johns Hopkins, nothing short of a miracle would make it possible for me to get in.

Less than a minute later, Dr. Han stepped into the room. "I will do your surgery in ten days. Be back here in one week for a complete physical. And by the way, we also want your doctor to do a complete physical on you before the surgery." This would be my third complete physical in less than a month!

Dr. Han went on to say that he was very proficient in the minimally invasive robotic DaVinci Method, but in my case would prefer to do the more extensive open procedure so he could get a better look at the surrounding tissues and lymph glands. It would be a three- to five-hour-long procedure. I immediately agreed, and signed the consent form. The fleece we had put down for God had been answered, and Dina and I walked out of that exam room praising God for His leading.

Our next stop was back to the receptionist—the woman who had first told me that Dr. Han never came in on Friday. "Mr. Schwartz," she said, "I have worked here for twenty-three years, and you have no idea how unusual this is. First, the doctors who work here do not call people back. That is my job. Second, Dr. Han has moved you to the top of his surgery schedule, and we are so busy here that to see a doctor only three days after you called is a miracle. The appointments we are making today are for consultations twelve weeks out! I don't know how Dr. Han managed to work you in. Third, and most unusual, if you are a nine, we normally would consider you terminal and not even let you into our program."

The receptionist stopped, as if considering how the impossible can be done so easily and then continued. "This is all happening so quickly that we will have to handwrite you into the surgery schedule. If I were to run you through the normal channels, your paperwork wouldn't be ready when you return. Here is your appointment card. I'll see you in a few days."

We left her office once again praising God for opening "unopenable" doors. As we made our way to our rental car, I wanted to sing! Here I was, oddly but quite possibly the happiest guy in the building, feeling secure in knowing that God was in control and that He had led us to this amazing doctor, a man who is one of the best prostate surgeons in the world and who works in one of the best prostate cancer hospitals in the world.

The next few days were a blur as we tried to get things caught up at home, went through another physical exam, scheduled airline flights and hotel rooms, and answered a thousand e-mails. Five days later, we were on another airliner, Johns Hopkins bound again.

Johns Hopkins is an amazing institution. It's huge—spread over many square miles and a dozen campuses. If it ceased to exist, so would Baltimore; it's the lifeblood of the city, providing hope and healing for thousands of residents in a city that has many varied personalities. The inner harbor is a bustling hotbed of activity—bands playing, jugglers juggling, and restaurants filling the air with delicious promises.

Other parts of the city, like the place where Sheree, our university-student daughter, could afford to live are littered with empty factories and brownstone houses whose boarded-up windows encourage you to walk faster.

Check-in at Johns Hopkins was quick and easy. Thirty minutes after our arrival I was in a ward with seventeen other men who were being prepped for the same kind of surgery I was having. Prostate cancer patients fill this room two to three times each weekday.

After a brief visit with my anesthetist, I lay down on a gurney and was whisked off to dreamland for three hours of surgery and two hours of waking up.

"Dad?" Our youngest daughter Terra's voice reached in through the fog. "Dad, did you know that your doctor is famous? I Googled him and found he has won a dozen awards and been published more than eighty times!"

About that time Dr. Han came into the recovery room. He said that the cancer had not been contained, but that he had taken as much extra tissue as he could. "There was still more that I couldn't get, Mr. Schwartz," he said apologetically. "I'm sorry."

In my groggy state I looked at him and said, "Dr. Han, I didn't know you were famous."

"Please," he said as he put both hands in front of his body as if to push my words away. "Anyone can get published. Let's not talk about it again. And please, to you I am not Dr. Han. Please call me Misop."

Dr. Han is much too formal. Here I was with this really amazing doctor who is not in the least bit pretentious or full of himself. This guy *REALLY* cares!

Misop arrived at my bedside at the crack of dawn, this time sitting on the end of the bed like a friend who isn't in a hurry. I asked him to tell me his side of the story of when we first talked over the phone.

"It was very unusual," Misop said. "Our receptionist had gone home for the night, so the supervisor took your call and was insistent that I call you back. I called you to make her happy, but also to tell you that you are terminal and we couldn't help you. Halfway through our phone conversation, I felt that I needed to help you. The next morning I came in and couldn't find a place on the schedule to fit you in, so I put you at the very top of the list. Last week I was off work to do house-shopping, and your surgery was the first I've done since I saw you ten days ago. I slipped you in at the front of the line. It was meant to be!"

Misop came to see me again the next morning, just as I was being discharged. He showed much concern over my future medical plans and handed me a card with his personal phone number on it. "Terry," he said, "if you ever want to talk, even if it isn't about cancer, call me." I thanked him, and he walked out the door.

That afternoon I received an e-mail from him saying that every month all of the cancer doctors get together to discuss the worst case they had seen that month. This month they would be talking about me. Mine was one of the most tumor-filled prostates they had ever dissected. "It looks," Misop said, "like you have been growing cancer for ten or fifteen years already."

As I pondered the words of my surgeon, I realized something that I should have years ago—only God has kept me alive.

CHAPTER 5

The Second Fleece

*I might have a stare-down with death, but I hear the Great Voice that says,
"Life begins when you do."*

I've discovered that it is always best to become as well acquainted with your disease as is possible. Learn what the scientific studies say. Be cautious of what you find on the Internet. My very best source for advice has been physician friends and networks that have cutting-edge research.

When you're on the Web, don't spend time on the sites that are encouraging you to try their miracle cure, but learn from the sites of large university hospitals, credible cancer organizations, and government health study centers. Then compare them all with each other so you know the right questions to ask your caregivers.

Most important of all, find a doctor you can talk to—one who knows your disease and is willing to listen to your crazy ideas and guide you to wise responses. If your doctor daydreams or checks his e-mail or plays with his putter while you're showing him studies you found at Johns Hopkins, Loma Linda, and Duke, find a new doctor.

I would also recommend that you get at least three opinions, in the hope that two of them will match up. If something doesn't feel right, keep looking. I was once asked by an oncologist why I had made an appointment with him. "You've been to five other oncologists already," he said. "Why are you here now?" Looking him squarely in the eye, I replied, "I'm looking for a doctor who is optimistic and aggressive." His response: "Be at the imaging center in one hour for scans." He is still my oncologist.

Some of the best advice I got came from a friend who had also battled cancer. He told me to make a game plan and stick with it and to avoid second guessing myself. He encouraged me to ask questions. And he said that nobody knows as much about how my body feels as I do, so I should listen to it and speak up if I believe we need to revisit the current plan of attack.

Your doctor should know your name and should want your spouse in the examination room with you. He or she should listen to you, answer your questions, admit what he doesn't know, recommend consultations with other specialists, and should call you the day after your visit "just to see how you're doing."

I also recommend that you find a masseuse who knows how to mitigate your pain. Massage can help patients deal with critical illnesses. Diet also plays a major role: we eat as much raw food as possible. Organic is another choice we feel is important.

One of the choices we made was to spend several weeks at Eden Valley Institute, a lifestyle center in the foothills of Colorado. I began with an eighteen-day program that included diet, exercise, hydrotherapy, and a daily IV of vitamin C and laetrile.

When we were nearing the end of our stay at Eden Valley, David Lopez called from Maranatha and asked us to go to India. Neither of us had any interest in going to India, so I asked if that assignment couldn't be changed to Africa. "We would *love* to go back to Africa!" I told him.

"No," David replied. "India is where we would like you to go next. We want you to supervise a construction project there."

I told him we would pray about it.

Dina and I talked about David's request. We were considering several options. Should we go back to Lincoln and stay away from international mission projects? Should I begin an aggressive chemotherapy program? Or should we say Yes to Maranatha and go on a mission trip to India? Not having a clear indication of what to do, we chose to put another fleece out before God just as Gideon had done long ago. If my life were a plane trip, we were asking God to sit in the pilot's seat and let us be copilots, or maybe even just flight attendants.

"Lord," we prayed, "we don't know what to do next. We realize that this is not a decision we should make on our own, so we're coming to You for specific guidance. We know You are with us and that You care about this decision even more than we do. We are coming to You as Gideon did so long ago, asking for a specific sign that will show us which way to go. If You want us to go to India, please have my cancer indicators be cut in half when we've completed our three-week stay at the health retreat center."

It was pretty audacious of us to put God on the spot, but we had felt God's leading when we laid out the first fleece, so why not put down a second one? Would God answer a second fleece? I was strongly impressed to ask in such a way that there were no gray areas—we needed the answer to be easy to discern.

During the next few days, I ate the best diet I could and increased the amount of exercise I was doing. And when I returned home from the health retreat center, a blood test showed that the cancer indicators had been cut *exactly in half*—not more nor less, but *exactly in half,* as we had asked. So I called David and told him that we were going to India. This would be the sixth Maranatha trip I went on since I had been diagnosed with terminal cancer.

We did go to India, but I've whipped myself a few times over how we tested God, how we asked Him for a sign. We pretty well knew that He would want us in India, so rather than asking for a 50 percent reduction in the PSA, maybe we should have asked Him to take the cancer completely away!

Did I not have enough faith to ask for the other 50 percent? How had I arrived at that number? All I can say is that we'd had more than one prayer session before we decided what our second fleece should be. I felt very strongly that we had chosen the right fleece. If God could cut my numbers in half, He could also keep me around as long as He desired.

All in all it was a very good fleece, as it clearly demonstrated who was in control—a God who loved me and was willing to guide me if I let Him. It gave me much confidence regarding my future. I realized again that He loves each of us as if we were the only one He loves.

CHAPTER 6

God's Rx for Healing

"A strong positive mental attitude will create more miracles than any wonder drug."

—Patricia Neal

I had chosen to place my decision about what to do next before God just as Gideon had on those soggy nights so long ago. My fleece had been the 50 percent reduction in the cancer indicators, and He gave me exactly what I asked for. He told me, "Go to India. Work as a construction supervisor for the Maranatha volunteers."

Since I was on a regular schedule of blood testing, I went in three weeks later for the regular blood draw my doctor had ordered. This blood test showed that my cancer had tripled in quantity and intensity. Now the science of cancer was looming over us again. God's sign was gone, and instead of being cut in half, my cancer had now tripled.

Looking at Dina, I questioned whether we should still go on the trip. "Changing our minds was not part of the deal we made with God," she responded. So, we finished packing and got on the plane for New Delhi. Maybe God was telling us that leading groups of volunteers on mission trips around the world was the perfect prescription for healing!

All the time we were in India, I thought about the 50 percent reduction fleece. Why had God made the numbers come out so perfectly? Was there something special in the IV I was given at the health retreat center? Should I go back there again? Dina and I talked it through thoroughly, and when we returned from India, I went back to Eden Valley for three more weeks of treatment.

When I had completed the treatment, I had my blood tested again, assuming that it would show another significant reduction in the cancer indicators. Instead, the testing showed that the cancer had tripled again. That proved to me that the first reduction had nothing to do with the IV medication; God had made it happen in response to my fleece. He really *had* wanted us to go to India! It was also something much bigger than that. It was an absolute indication of who had control of my disease, and it certainly wasn't me.

One of my commitments from day one of this war has been "quantity over quality." That's one reason I began the hormone therapy. My type of cancer feeds on testosterone, so I may be able to slow the disease by eliminating testosterone, which "gets me in touch with my feminine side." It is a continual challenge as my body struggles to keep up with my mind. The therapy I'm getting makes me feel much worse than the cancer does. It takes away my energy, my stamina. That's the price I have to pay in exchange for possibly being around a bit longer. I think it's a good trade-off, but that is my choice. I can certainly understand other people choosing to go in another direction.

The bottom line is that being able to slow down the cancer is *really* a good thing. However, for that to happen, you have to do some terrible things that make you feel really bad. My mind tells me to keep planning for years to come, but my body says, "Wow, that last trip was fun! How many more do you think you have in you?"

Life is really a balancing act . . .

My mind has so many other questions:

+ As a cancer patient, how should I balance faith and medicine?
+ I know I'm in a war and the enemy wants to win. What role does God play along the way, and how does He define victory?
+ If I truly believe that God can and will heal me, why am I still consulting with physicians?
+ Am I to wait on God for healing, or does He expect me to get my life together so He can act?
+ Some of the treatments modern medicine offers will make me feel worse. Should I follow the doctor's advice and use them?

God doesn't want me to sit on my hands waiting for Him to act. I certainly have to get my lifestyle in order. There's a chance that some of my lifestyle choices may have gotten me into this situation in the first place, and now would be a very good time to be sure I'm living as healthfully as possible. Today's choices may improve my body's immune system and give God a better body to work with.

Dina and I have been getting all kinds of divergent advice on what to do next, so we've decided to become our own counselors while also accepting the help of many a friend. This is not a route I would suggest for everyone, but we chose this path and it works for us.

There are two schools of thought. One is to follow the advice and practice of mainstream modern medicine by attacking the cancer with surgery, chemicals, and radiation. This approach often saves lives, but the treatments often bring the patients to death's door. The other school of thought says cancer victims should take the "holistic" route, which focuses on building the immune system through diet and lifestyle changes.

As you know from what I've told you so far in this book, we've chosen a bit of both. Our plan has been to use the best we can find in both approaches, but to refuse to do chemo. If there were even a 1 percent chance that chemo would cure me, I would rethink my position. But with prostate cancer, chemo only buys a bit more time, and not a good quality of time at that. It also destroys one's immune system.

My cancer had progressed to a Gleason score of 9.0, meaning that from a human viewpoint, I was at the end of my rope. Dr. Han heard my urgent request, and God impressed him to perform surgery, even though doing so might hurt his statistics of success. So, Dr. Han removed my prostate surgically at Johns Hopkins University Medical Center.

We have also carefully reviewed our lifestyle choices and made many changes in how we live. We have revised our diet; we're eating more organic foods and as much raw food as possible. We have significantly reduced or eliminated our use of sugar, milk, cheese, and red meats. I've also begun drinking alkaline water, because some people say cancer can't live in an alkaline environment. In the first few months after my diagnosis, I took more than twenty-five supplements three times a day. Now I am down to just two, both of which boost the immune system.

However, I believe God really deserves all the credit for my still being here. It is He and He alone who sustains all of us. One of my favorite prayers when I awake in the morning says, "God, thank You for this day. Help me to give it back to You."

CHAPTER 7

An Evening in Xai-Xai

Some of God's best gifts must be unwrapped in the dark.

Waking up at 4:15 A.M. is hard to do unless you are living on the Indian Ocean. That makes it easy—the sunrises are spectacular. It was a good ten-minute walk down to the water's edge, and 4:30 is when the sun would make its grand entrance, orange shimmers dancing on the ocean's ripples on the coast of Mozambique.

By 5:15 we were diving headlong into the surf, getting cooled off for the morning and also getting our exercise. The undertow was fierce; we later learned that each year several people die right where we were swimming because they underestimate the fury of the surf. And it was true: the waves were breaking hard on the shore, picking us up and rolling us in the water and sand before spitting us out on the beach.

Xai-Xai was the first project we went on after I was diagnosed. We were there to build three churches. David was our leader. He couldn't have chosen a better place to stay. Waking up to the Indian Ocean is certainly something I could get used to.

Friday night the entire team of volunteers assembled at Mama Clara's church. When we arrived, we discovered that the evening was going to be far different than we had expected. We had assumed that we would have a small meal of fruit and then sing a few songs, tell a few stories, and have a prayer of dedication for the work we had done during the past two weeks.

Instead, when we walked in the back door of the church, we found ourselves in a mini–upper room. The inside walls were lined with fancy new wooden benches that had been donated to the church by the Gates Forming company in Denver, Colorado, and in the center there was a low table absolutely overflowing with fruit and vegetables and nuts. What made it extra special was that David and his crew had set the tables in the shape of a cross and had placed small candles in paper bags that echoed that shape. The arrangement was so moving that Dina and I both felt lumps in our throats.

David played his violin, and we sang a few songs. Then Pastor Dick shared a short message about love and service. I don't remember much of that because I had begun to realize the program wasn't really about celebrating the work our team had done in Xai-Xai. No, they had come together to pray for Dina and me. That was overwhelming.

What I remember most about the evening was that they asked us to come to the center of the room, and then everyone gathered around us, put their hands on us, and prayed for us. There is nothing more powerful in the whole world than the feeling that comes when you know you're being prayed for. Sure, we all pray often.

Dina and I pray constantly for patience, for kindness, for hope, and for healing. But to have nearly a hundred friends stand around us, make a prayer-touch chain that connected us all, and then to hear prayer after prayer lifting the two of us before God's throne . . . Well, the memory still takes our breaths away.

Someone asked me what has given me the most hope since I was diagnosed with cancer. I think they expected me to talk about some awesome book I had read or an e-mail someone had written to me. None of that matches knowing that I am being prayed for. *That is the greatest gift anyone can give me!*

Sunrise over the Indian Ocean near Xai-Xai, Mozambique.

BEGINNINGS

"Life must be lived forward, but can only be understood backwards."

—Søren Kierkegaard

CHAPTER 8

Life on the Prairie

*"Cherish your yesterdays, dream your tomorrows, and live your todays.
Tomorrow belongs to those who fully use today."*

—Unknown

My mother was raised on a farm in North Dakota. There were five children in the family. She and my dad got married when she was young—just nineteen. I remember her as a very petite brunette with sparkling blue-green eyes and a musical laugh.

When I was born, my parents were living in Lincoln, Nebraska, but we soon moved to Hemmingford, where my dad had gotten a job teaching school. It seems really weird, but even though I wasn't in school yet, I can remember practically every day I lived there in Hemmingford. I'd go to school with my dad, sit in the back row, and pretend that I was a student.

Mom was an excellent cook. I'm especially thankful that we have her recipes for cottage cheese roast, German chocolate cake, and mint chocolate brownies.

My folks lived a pretty simple life until 1957, when they bought a TV. That was a really big deal back then. Hardly anyone had televisions, especially among our fundamentalist church friends, who believed that televisions would bring the devil right into your house! Mom and Dad thought it over and bought a TV. We didn't watch it much because the rabbit ears could only bring in stations that were nearby, and there weren't many stations near Hemmingford.

Then one evening Mom and Dad caught Bruce and me hiding behind the couch and watching *Gunsmoke* with them over their shoulders. They were so upset that they sold the TV and didn't get another one until I had graduated from high school.

When we first moved to Hemmingford, we lived in a little white frame house beside an Indian reservation. Unfortunately, we never really got to know any of the Indians because we feared them. Our impressions of them were that they drank a lot of alcohol, and they beat their drums at night when we were trying to sleep. I've often wondered what would have happened if we had taken some of Mom's great brownies to the reservation and given them away to the Indians. My guess is that I would have made some lifelong friends there rather than just fear-filled memories.

When I was five, old enough for kindergarten, we moved to Shelton, Nebraska, where Dad had been offered a job building boats at Platte Valley Academy. So, while Mom taught piano, organ, and choir, Dad started a boat factory. He made boats from fiberglass and plywood—boats designed for families to use for water-skiing and dads to use for fishing. I rather doubt that the boat business ever made much money, but it did provide work for some of the students, and it provided a lot of fun for Bruce and me.

Dad had to test each boat before he sold it. That was where the fun came for us boys. Mom would bake cookies and fill the cooler with tomato sandwiches and punch. The student workers would bring their girlfriends, and we'd all climb in whatever vehicle was towing the boat for an hour of bouncing down the road to the lake. Then, as Harold, one of the student workers, says, "We skied the lake up." I wasn't old enough to ski, but I could ride in the boat, and could eat a lot of cookies!

My parents were sponsors of the senior class, and some Friday nights we had the members of that class over to our house for waffles and ice cream. I really looked forward to those evenings because that was my bonus time. That's when I got to mix with the students and make lifelong friends.

My friend-making skill paid off at other times too. On many Sundays, late afternoons, and weekends, the "big people" would take me with them flying model airplanes, roller-skating, and other things that "big people" do. When you're six, or seven, or eight years old, that's pretty cool stuff.

My mother had a couple of treasures in our living room—a small, walnut-colored spinet piano and a genuine Hammond organ, the church model. She was proud of both of them, but she played the organ most. I loved listening to her play, especially when she played from memory. Listening to her play was like having my own private concert.

Mom wanted both Bruce and me to take piano lessons, but she didn't think it would be wise for her to be our teacher. She said that she was afraid that she might not have enough patience to love us through the learning, so she sent us over to another of the faculty wives. That woman tried to teach us to play, but I disliked every minute of it and never learned much more than where middle C is.

We stayed at Platte Valley for three years, and then something happened that has helped me understand service, caring, and the value of family like nothing else could have. My grandparents, Dad's parents, lived in North Dakota. Their farm was large, and the winters were hard, especially for folks who were growing older and more vulnerable to winter's arthritic challenges. For several years, my grandparents had rented a small apartment in Lincoln during the coldest months.

During that season, they couldn't do anything on the farm anyway, so they moved south to Nebraska, away from the twenty-foot-high snowdrifts.

I know, they should have gone to Florida or the Bahamas or some other logical snowbird destination. But they loved Lincoln and had family there. I guess we warmed their lives more than humid Florida would have.

Trouble was, when they went home that last year, they found that their house had been burglarized, and everything was gone. Everything! They called my dad and told him the story. Dad is a caring, loving guy who has always been willing to step out for others, even when it was costly to him. He has helped me see that helping others is what God wants us to do. He offered to move my grandparents to Lincoln and build them a house where they could live all year round. So we moved to Lincoln to care for Dad's parents, and Dad, who had already built a couple small homes, became a full-time builder.

The house Dad built for my grandparents was very nice—Dad had even built a small apartment in the basement that they could rent out so they would have a regular income. People noticed how well the house was built, and they began lining up to have Dad build a Schwartz home for them too. The second house he built in Lincoln, over on 51st and Meredith, now has eight other Schwartz houses around it.

Unfortunately, the winter of our second year in Lincoln, my mom was diagnosed as having cancer. At first it was only in her breasts, but then it spread throughout her body. The next three-and-a-half years were really hard—a time of constant waiting, wondering, hoping, and trying to keep on living regardless.

And then she died.

CHAPTER 9

When Mom Left

"Kites rise highest against the wind, not with it."

—Winston Churchill

Mom died when I was twelve. God abandoned me that day. At least, that's what I thought.

Mom was thirty-two when she died. I knew she was a really good woman who had strong health principles. She didn't smoke. She didn't drink. Not even pop. Well, maybe a 7-Up. That was about as bad as she got. No coffee. No meat. A vegetarian all her life.

She had been anointed and prayed for, and as a kid, I really believed that she would be healed. We were raised to believe that. So when it didn't happen, I felt that God had let me down. Not the doctors. Not anyone else. It was God who had let me down. I didn't tell Him that. I really didn't even know how to tell Him what I was feeling, what I was thinking.

I wondered why God would do this to my dad. He had his hands full—he had three kids to raise. I had no idea why God would let bad things happen to good people. All I knew was that if you loved God, He did good things for you. That was my faith, and it came directly from my folks and my grandparents.

My grandparents were *Schwartzes* from the old country. Though they spoke English, they also spoke German, especially when they had something to say and didn't want us to hear what they were talking about.

They were good people. Even though they never made a lot of money and consequently were very frugal, there were times when that frugality went out the window. Like when Grandma would take us to the store. She would always say, "Is there anything you want? Put it in the grocery bag." It could be ice cream. It could be candy. Or even a pair of blue jeans. It didn't matter what it was. If we wanted something, she wanted us to have it, and she would buy it for us.

From the time I was in grade four till I was in grade seven, we lived right next door to them. We got a lot of affirmation then. We did a lot of things together. Granddad had a sledgehammer and a few wedges, so we'd go out in the backyard and split wood. They also had a large garden, and we pulled weeds and hoed. After we had done the chores, Grandma would always give us *kuchen* or fruit strudels—treats she made that we couldn't get anywhere else. They also had a TV, and they'd let us watch *Petticoat Junction* and *The Rifleman* and sometimes even *The Lone Ranger.*

Granddad and Grandma were two of the hardest-working people I've known. By 6:00 A.M. Granddad had already walked several miles just getting warmed up for the day. His hands made my hands look like new. They were wrinkled and worn from years and years of working outside on the farm, in the garden, and keeping Dad's construction sites cleaned up. He enjoyed going to work.

Granddad's been gone about twenty-five years now, and Grandma's been gone a dozen or so. We still miss them. Family is really all we have. It's everything.

I went to College View Academy my freshman year and had a great time. I liked the kids, had great teachers, and wasn't called into the principal's office even once. They hardly knew I existed. I spent all my time in the library, reading books. It was good.

But after that very good year, I left home and went to Platte Valley Academy. Dad had remarried, and my stepmother and I weren't getting along. I liked our house. I liked my room. I loved the library. I liked Lincoln. I was OK with school, the kids, and the teachers. I even got along well with my stepsisters! But it was time for me to move on.

So I went to Platte Valley Academy in Shelton, Nebraska, despite the fact that I had no friends there. They even had to assign me a roommate! But God certainly had His hand in the change of schools. PVA was the perfect place for me, and my roommate Neil was the perfect friend.

Neil and I did things that we shouldn't have, but we didn't do things that were really bad. The problem was that the faculty saw us as trouble, so they blamed us for most everything that went wrong on campus—even the things we didn't do.

The boys' dormitory was very old and had incredibly thick walls. In fact, some of the walls were so thick that there was room for teenage guys to make a passageway between the inside and outside of those walls. We devised a way to slip through them from one end of the dorm nearly to the other end.

Having access to that hidden passageway made it possible for us to surreptitiously rig power for our transistor radio and cassette tape deck, neither of which dormitory students were supposed to have. We removed the plaster behind the baseboard in our closet and built a little safe for our contraband, and then we ran a wire through the passageway directly into the main fuse panel. That way we had power even after Stan turned the lights out at 10:00 P.M., and we could listen to whatever music we wanted to whenever we wanted to.

After two up-and-down years behavior- and reputation-wise, the school asked me not to come back for my senior year. At that point, Harry Riley, one of my former teachers, stepped in. He agreed to help me get back into PVA. After considerable pleading and promising on my part, the faculty allowed me to return. But rather than letting me back in the dorm, they said I had to live with one of the faculty families.

So I moved in with the maintenance man and lived in the basement of his house with his brother Tom. That was when I became acquainted with dynamite-and-oxyacetylene bombs. Thanks, Tom, for the education! We used to grin at each other when people talked about all the sonic booms they'd begun to hear.

It was about this time that two incidents—or more to the point, two accidents—occurred in which I should have seen God's presence and His love. The first started with Neil and me on a "borrowed" motorbike and two blinding headlights burning into my head. Guessing that meant there was a car headed toward me in my lane, I laid the motorbike over just as the lights and the vehicle they were on smashed into us.

Seconds earlier, we'd been cruising down a rural Nebraska highway. Now we were sliding on the asphalt toward a 1968 Impala that was also powering its way toward us. The combined speeds at impact added up to well over one hundred miles per hour.

It was a Saturday night, and Neil and I, boarding students at Platte Valley Academy, had been heading into town—which, of course, was a violation of the school's rules. It seemed like a good idea when we climbed onto Steve's Bridgestone motorbike that night and without permission rode off campus to play a game of pool. Was either of us any good at pool? Not at all. But that wasn't really the reason we were going off campus. We were going because we were just plain bored. Listening to a band rehearsal didn't really sound like much fun.

So we were on our way to town when we saw the car coming toward us. The driver, who was drunk, was drawn to our light and veered into our lane. Seeing that a crash was inevitable, I laid the motorbike over and we both kicked away from it as hard as we could. Then the front bumper whacked us, and the car seemed to suck us under it. There was a quick series of thumps as both wheels on the passenger's side of the car ran over Neil's and my legs. I thought being run over by a car would hurt a lot worse than it did. We had tire tracks on our knees, a shoelace broken in five places, and Neil, my passenger, roommate, and oft-time partner in crime had a broken ankle to prove that it really had happened.

As I was sliding down the highway, a few things ran through my mind. I noticed that the asphalt was really smooth, that our encounter with the car hadn't hurt as much as I expected—and that the semitractor-trailer coming straight at us was really big! We slid into the ditch just before it roared by. So far, so good—except, what would the school say?

When my folks lived in Shelton, they had become friends with Mike Ryan—owner of the Conoco station. Now I needed Mike's help. The drunk had pulled over and was crying, thinking that he was going to jail for killing two guys on a motorcycle. Mike had lived in Shelton long enough to know that the school we were attending had some pretty strict rules, so he helped us out the best way he knew how. Folding a five-dollar bill and putting it in the drunk's pocket, he said, "Henry, go buy yourself some more beer and then go home. The boys are fine, don't worry about them." With that we picked up the motorbike, went to the pool hall, and played our game of pool.

Then we were asked to leave because we were bleeding just a bit and our clothes looked really scuffed up. The plan was to say that Neil had fallen down a flight of stairs. That plan fell apart two days later, when the drunk sobered up and called the school to see how the boys that he hit were doing. Our parents were notified and were at the school to pick us up before we knew we were in trouble.

All my buddies back at the high school in Lincoln were getting wheels, some of which were pretty cool, like a '68 455 HO Firebird and a '63 Impala. Others were getting motorcycles, and it was on one of those that I used up another of my cat lives.

We had pulled out of the school parking lot on Doug's new 350 Scrambler. I was just turning my head to let him know we were hitting 70 miles per hour, in case he couldn't see the needle, when a station wagon backed out into the street and stopped. It was blocking the entire road, and we weren't going to be able to stop, so we followed the bike, which was throwing up a big stream of sparks, under the car on one side and out the other.

How we fit without hitting anything I still don't know. What I do remember is that we both were wearing tennis shoes and cutoffs, and that's all. No helmet. Nothing for safety. The asphalt was super rough right there. It ground my wallet in half, and it ground through Doug's too—and then wore a hole in his butt. The last time I saw him, he reminded me of that. We slid more than fifty yards, dusted ourselves off, and moved on. As I look back now, I realize that there had to have been Someone looking out for me in both instances—just as there is now.

CHAPTER 10

Life After School

We can't avoid rejection, but we can choose how we'll respond to it.

I had always dreamed of being a medical doctor, so my senior year at PVA I tried my best to excel in the science classes. The chemistry instructor, Harold Williams, was an outstanding teacher. He could explain hard things in a way a farm boy could understand them, and he nurtured my love of science. I did go to college for a couple years—until I realized that I would never be able to afford medical school. Then I put that dream aside.

Meanwhile, Dina and I had become an item. In time, I managed to work up enough courage to ask her dad for her hand in marriage. Much to my chagrin, his answer was a resounding *"No!"* Two days later, I got an official, four-page rejection letter from him, carefully detailing why we shouldn't marry. Among his other complaints, he listed the fact that my last name started with the letter *S,* just like Charles Starkweather's last name—and he was a mass murderer! I still have that letter, and every now and then I dig it out to remind me that rejection is a part of life. We can't avoid it—but we can choose how we'll respond to it.

When Dina and I arrived at the ripe old age of twenty, we felt that life was passing us by, so we decided to get married. The years that followed were really good ones. We didn't have much money, but we had each other, and nothing else mattered much!

Fortunately, Dina loved drag racing as much as I did, so we spent large parts of our paychecks on "go-fast" parts for our 1968 Camaro, and we spent every Sunday at a track somewhere, burning fuel and rubber. We won some races and we lost some—and eventually we realized that *race car* is simply another name for *bottomless, money-sucking pit.*

We waited six years before enlarging our family. During that time, I worked for my dad as a carpenter, and Dina worked at St. Elizabeth's as a nurse.

I still had a lot of issues to sort out with God, but I didn't know just how one goes about doing that. During those years, I lived like a Christian, but I left most of God's power on the shelf. Dina and I ran a Pathfinder club, led in the youth division, and taught Sabbath School classes. I was a deacon and an elder. But my religion just wasn't as real as it could have been. I was serving a God who had really let me down, and at times I wondered whether He would eventually let us down again. Instead of making a real commitment to Him, I put half my eggs in His basket and kept the other half in my own basket.

I'm sure we can't really divide our loyalties like that, but we find many ways to delude ourselves into believing we can be in charge and still serve God. Sometimes it seems to work, but it isn't God's plan.

CHAPTER 11

Life Changes

"We cannot achieve our wildest dreams by remaining who we are."

—John C. Maxwell

I had a Seamco resurfacing business for twenty years. We resurfaced driveways, patios, swimming pools, and just about anything that had deteriorating concrete. Those years were very good, but also very stressful. We were always dealing with deadlines. Always rushed; always going from a job site in Lincoln to one in Omaha and then to Grand Island for another. I had good guys working for me, and we were respected for turning out high-quality work, but doing this business in Nebraska was challenging. Often, it was either too hot or too cold—which made for a very stressful situation when we had just one shot at installing thousands of dollars' worth of product correctly. A little untimely rainstorm or some sprinklers accidently turned on would ruin everything. It wasn't the type of job where we could sit down and take a break. Once we started applying the product, there was no stopping for a rest.

A longtime employee who was also my right-hand man ended up with the business. The customers didn't even have to learn a new name. A *Terry* still very successfully owns and runs it. But my family all appreciated it when my life calmed down.

This was a time of one of my greatest regrets. I was trying to be a good dad by working hard to provide for my girls. But I was working too much and not spending enough time with my rapidly growing daughters. About that time, the girls finished high school and moved on to college, so life around the house was a bit slower. These changes gave me a chance to sit down, look clearly at my life, and decide who I wanted to be.

Some people might say, "Oh, Terry got sick and then he changed."

I don't think that's true. I started changing long before I learned I had cancer. The disease just gave me an even better reason to live as I hoped God wanted me to live. For too many years I'd had a type A personality. It's not a disease; it's a personality type. Being very time conscious and competitive, and multitasking to accomplish more is often just part of it. Having a low tolerance of incompetence is another part. That is something I've had to work very hard on. Many a time I've been a little too quick to give my opinion. Now I try to listen. I learn so much more that way.

If I could relive some of those days as the person God is making me become today, I know I would have been more helpful and understanding than I was.

What would I do today, and why would it be different?

That's hard to say. I think I have become a much more patient person. I know I'm learning to think of others first and myself last. But it's not always easy. If I didn't start every day by asking God to plan my schedule, take over my emotions, and give me peace, I'd probably still be the same old Terry.

CHAPTER 12

A World of Hurt

"You never know how strong you are, until being strong is the only choice you have."

—Unknown

This story starts when my grandmother's brother, Uncle Lloyd, came to live with my grandparents for a few months. Terra really liked Uncle Lloyd. He was kind to her, and he liked to play games and was just generally a lot of fun.

While he was staying with my grandparents, Uncle Lloyd caught pneumonia and was put in the hospital's intensive care unit. After a couple days, the hospital agreed to let Grandma bring Terra along to visit her great-granduncle in the intensive care unit (the ICU). When they came into his room, he was unconscious and hooked up to all kinds of machines, with tubes coming out of his nose and mouth. It wasn't a pretty picture for a young girl to store in her memory.

Unfortunately, three days later Uncle Lloyd died.

Terra was devastated.

Just a few months later—two days before Dina's fortieth birthday—our world suffered a near knockout blow. The girls had just come home from school, and Dina, who was seven months pregnant, was getting them ready for their after-school activities—tennis, swimming, and track. After about twenty minutes of clothes-changing and collecting sports gear, they got back into the car. By then it was about five o'clock, and what had been a light rain had become a freezing drizzle that was coating Lincoln's streets with black ice.

Dina was following a car down 56th Street, and two vehicles were coming toward her in the other lane: a car and an ancient, fifteen-passenger van. Suddenly, the woman driving the van decided to pass the car in front of her. She made it around that car and managed to miss the car in front of Dina too, but then her big, old van with its slick tires and not a lick of insurance slammed head-on into Dina's car.

The cops estimated that each vehicle was going fifty miles per hour or more when they hit, and they struck each other so dead-on that they didn't even slide; they just smashed into each other and then bounced back about five inches. The ice they were on was so slick that a person couldn't even walk on it.

Dina remembers that a woman opened the door of her car—a woman she was sure was an angel. The woman surveyed the situation quickly and then dashed across the street to her home and returned to the car with towels and blankets.

The force of the crash had thrown Dina into the steering wheel of the car, bending it way back. And somehow the femur in one of her legs had been broken, and now that leg was twisted clear back on itself and it was bleeding badly.

Terra had smashed into the dashboard face-first and was screaming bloody screams. And Dina was sure that Sheree was dead. Her eyes were rolled back in her head; she looked lifeless, and Dina couldn't rouse her.

Because of the black ice, it took the first ambulance that arrived at the site of the accident more than an hour to get there—covering a distance that normally would have taken just ten minutes. It was a miracle that neither Terra nor Dina had bled out.

Dina refused to go in that first ambulance; insisting instead, with selfless love, that the girls go first. Eventually, another ambulance came and brought Dina to the emergency room.

Meanwhile, I was downtown at a home show, trying to keep our construction business going. Someone came and told me there'd been an accident and that I should go to Lincoln General Hospital as soon as I could and meet the ambulance at the emergency room. I was terrified and wanted to be with Dina immediately, but the roads were basically impassable. I went as fast as was possible in those conditions, but it still took me twenty minutes to drive less than two miles.

When I got to the emergency room, the ambulance was still in transit. I stood around, went outside to look, and generally stewed for another hour and a half, waiting for the ambulance to arrive and wondering who was hurt and how badly. The questions kept circling through my mind: *Are they alive? Should I wait here, or should I go out where they are? What can I do? What's happening?* We had cell phones, but mine was hardwired into my truck, and Dina's was in the crashed car. It was a crazy and traumatic night.

But as bad as it was for me, it was even worse for Dina. She's a nurse, so when the EMTs (emergency medical technicians) finally got to her and began tearing off her clothes and started to put a tube down her nose, she came unglued and started barking, "No, I don't want an NG tube! You're not putting that down me! Don't hold my hands."

When the ambulances finally arrived, I wanted to know immediately everyone's condition, and then I started to tell everyone what to do. I think the ER nurses wanted to medicate me as much as they wanted to medicate Dina, who was crying and demanding and still in so much pain that all they wanted to do with her was move her into surgery—*now!* But the doctor hadn't arrived yet.

Dina had three fractured ribs, which were causing her unbearable pain; her right leg was nothing more than a mass of exploded bones; her ankle was the size of a volleyball and as black as a coal miner's face; she was seven months pregnant, and they knew they were going to have to do a C-section right away.

Two terrible hours later, the doctor finally arrived. He took a quick look at all three of my girls and then rolled Dina off to surgery, where he delivered the baby and put a Steinman pin in Dina's leg. That pin would enable them to hold her leg in traction until the swelling went down and the surgeon could put a steel rod in her leg.

My heart was in my shoes, and my hopes were full of cracks as I watched the nurses roll Dina away. What was happening to us? What was going to happen to our son? Where was God in all of this?

But there wasn't time to worry about the big questions. I had two daughters who needed their dad. I started with Terra.

When Terra's ambulance arrived at the hospital, they immediately put her right where she needed to be, in the place where they could best help her—the intensive care unit. Unfortunately, that was the place where Uncle Lloyd died. Not until several years later did we realize that when our seven-year-old baby saw that she was in the place where Uncle Lloyd died, she knew she was going to die too.

Terra's face had ploughed directly into the dashboard of our bright-red Oldsmobile Toronado, smashing her whole jaw into tiny fragments. When she arrived in ICU, the medical team there had to tie her down because she wanted to tear out all the tubes and the mouthpiece and run from the Room of Certain Death. I spent almost twenty-four hours at her bedside, sometimes dashing down to the adult ICU to see Dina and then rushing back to be with Terra again. She was alive, alert, in terrible pain, certain that she was going to die—and her mouth was wired shut, which meant that she couldn't talk.

The hospital had given us a small chalkboard so Terra could communicate with us. No doubt there were a lot of questions she would have liked to ask. But she couldn't have fit them on that board—even if she could have spelled them.

At one point she motioned to me that she would be calm and leave the tubes alone if they would just release her arms for a few moments. Eventually, we all agreed and the restraints were loosened. Terra immediately grabbed all of the tubes and ripped them out of her nose, mouth, and arms. One of those tubes ran to a device that was inflated in her mouth to hold the broken bones in place. It's not hard to imagine the excruciating pain she must have felt when she pulled that device out of her mouth. What she did to herself caused almost as much trauma as the accident itself did. In fact, it did so much additional damage that nearly everything constricted shut with new swelling.

It was a very dark time for all of us. I don't think I left the hospital for five days. I'd sleep in Dina's room for thirty minutes, go upstairs and spend three or four hours with Terra, check on Sheree, and then go back down to Dina. That first week was very long, dark, and horrible.

Sheree was the most fortunate one. All she had was a concussion, so she was able to go home after just a couple days. She couldn't play tennis for a while, and that upset her, but otherwise she pulled through fine.

Not so Dina.

The hospital administrators didn't allow us to choose our surgeon; instead, they assigned us to the one on call when she arrived at the hospital. That happened to be the one surgeon in Lincoln that Dina had told me she never wanted to see again. In her nursing work, she had met many physicians; some professional and kind, and others mediocre and careless. This doctor was *not* her choice, but she was rolled into his surgery anyway.

Yes, her leg hurt, her head hurt, and her ankle was beyond pain, but worst of all, during the two hours she was waiting for the doctor to come, she was feeling the life of our unborn son slowly slip away.

When the doctor finally did arrive, he performed the C-section right away and delivered a baby boy who still had a heartbeat. But the baby survived only a couple hours. Both of us believe that if the doctor had left his sports event when he was called rather than waiting a while and then coming slowly, we would have a son now.

It's interesting that the period at the end of that last sentence looks so small and insignificant, yet it is one of the largest mountains Dina and I have had to climb together. We really wanted a son. We had hoped for a son. We had dreamed of a son. We had picked a name for him, and had even planned activities that we could do with two girls and a boy. Now we'd had a son, and he was gone. Nothing can describe our pain adequately. It was a black night.

Then the three teachers showed up.

At about 11:30 P.M., three of our girls' teachers walked through the door. Kathy Bollinger, Linda Reitsma, and Cherie Hauck came to see how we were doing. They were so worried about us that despite the icy streets, they came to pour their love into our hearts! They were like bright, calming angels in our really dark night.

The next day a hospital psychiatrist bounced into Dina's room with a big, happy smile and said, "Good morning! Well, how do you feel?"

I thought Dina would punch him out, but she had too many tubes, cords, and wires holding her back. Instead, in tones that nearly scorched the room, she said, "Just how do you think I feel?"

We didn't have a very good time with this man, and when he left—more quickly than he had come—Dina called the nurse and told her to "never let that guy come back into my room again! Never!"

Dina just couldn't believe that he could come in and ask such an inconsiderate, unfeeling question. Hadn't he read Dina's chart? Didn't he know that we had lost our baby son and that both our daughters were hospitalized?

I seconded Dina's demand.

The day after the accident, one of our friends, Donell Martinez, a nurse who worked at the hospital, asked us if we would like to see our son and hold him. She was an awesome mother and nurse and knew exactly what Dina and I needed right then. Yes, it was a little weird to touch and hold a dead baby, but it was something we needed.

Pastor Greg, the pastor of our home church in College View, came to the hospital a few times, and he held a funeral for the baby there in the hospital. That was a very sad event. Terra was still in the ICU, but Sheree and I were there, along with other family members, and the nurses wheeled Dina in on a stretcher so she could be at our son's funeral. All of that time is a gray blur to me now.

Both Terra and Dina were in the hospital for nearly two weeks—two very long weeks of praying and watching IVs drip and checking ICU monitors. Since Terra was in the ICU, no one could send her flowers. So instead, they sent stuffed animals. By the time she was discharged, she had a furry menagerie of more than fifty stuffed animals: Purple unicorns. Brown, black, and honey-colored bears. Dogs, cats, lions, and zebras. She could have started a zoo! I really choked up one afternoon when I came into Terra's room and found a banner hanging over her bed. All of the kids at school had worked on an immense "Get Well, Terra, We Miss You" banner that was so huge it nearly filled the room. Her entire class even visited on a field trip when she was out of ICU.

Terra was in the ICU for nearly a week and then in another unit for several more days, till she was well enough for us to care for her at home. When I brought her home from the hospital, her mouth was completely wired shut so it would heal straight. The only way she could eat was through a straw. During that time, Dina was on crutches and wasn't able to cook; our lives were touched by the kindness showed us by so many through the food they brought our family. Terra's first-grade teacher brought her own blender to school to help us by making all of Terra's lunches. She made soups and other foods that could be blended. Terra has told us that now that she is a teacher herself, she has used the love extended to her by her first-grade teacher—and other people too—as a model of how to relate to her kids.

Because the medical team was so worried that something would go wrong with Terra's orthodontic harness, they sent an emergency call button along with her. "Carry this everywhere," they told her, "and if anything breaks or begins to feel like it is out of place, push this button, and one of us will come over to help you." Terra found that it was harder to remember to carry the button than it was to go to school and be normal.

When Terra flew into the dashboard, she lost six teeth, four of them permanent teeth. Our dentist took this as a challenge and made a temporary plate that she could wear so she wouldn't look like someone from *Li'l Rascals*. That was great, but that temporary plate was also a pain. Terra had to take it out several times a day to wash and disinfect it, which was hard work for a seven-year-old! On top of that, she couldn't eat some foods that were among her favorites, such as apples and corn on the cob. But did she ever complain about the inconveniences and restrictions? Nope. Not even once. She is an amazing trooper.

I still can't believe that she never complained, especially since her dental surgeons weren't able to do the final reconstruction of her mouth and jaw and give her permanent teeth again until nearly fifteen years after the accident. It took all that time to implant enough bone to hold her teeth. Fifteen years is a long time to wait, but through it all she never complained.

Three days after the crash, I went out to look at the car. After all, that's what a husband—especially a husband who races cars—would do. I wanted to see our Toronado, kick the tires, and thank God that all three of my girls got out alive.

When I saw the car, I couldn't understand how anyone survived. I found some of Terra's teeth stuck in the dashboard. It looked like she had decided the dash was a giant piece of watermelon and had bit into it so hard that her teeth had gotten stuck in it and stayed there—along with little shards of jawbone—when she removed the piece. It was ugly, really ugly. I knelt beside the Toronado and prayed a long soggy prayer of thanksgiving.

Two days after the accident, on Dina's fortieth birthday, she had an operation. Her birthday present was a steel rod that the surgeon put in her leg so she would be able to walk again someday.

When she was wheeled out of the recovery room, she had tubes and IVs everywhere, but she was able to grunt a greeting to the family members who were waiting to wish her a happy birthday. All she could say in reply was, "I truly know what it feels like to be over the hill." Then one of the nurses gave her a tiny bit of vanilla ice cream. That was a small promise that eventually things would be better.

When Dina was released, her foot, which was still black-and-blue from the crash, was hurting terribly. We took her to a doctor, who had some X-rays made. They showed that her ankle was still a mass of bone fragments. The doctors at the hospital had worried so much about her leg that they had missed her ankle!

Upon seeing those X-rays, this doctor said, "We need to operate on your ankle right away."

"Oh no you don't!" Dina responded. "I've had enough surgeries to last my lifetime. I'm not having any more!"

ROADS LESS TRAVELED

*"Today well lived makes every yesterday a dream of happiness,
and every tomorrow a vision of hope."*

—Sanskrit Proverb

*"May your trails be crooked, winding, lonesome, dangerous, leading to the
most amazing view. May your mountains rise into and above the clouds."*

—Edward Abbey

CHAPTER 13

The Pathways Kids

"Try not to become a man of success but rather to become a man of value."

—Albert Einstein

Stewart Bainum, who made his fortune in nursing homes and hotels, dreamed of helping to educate children—especially those who otherwise didn't have a fair shot at life. To accomplish this, Mr. Bainum established the Commonweal Foundation, which has dedicated most of its funds to schools, teachers, and students.

In 1995, the foundation decided to try a new approach to helping inner-city teenagers whose lives were falling apart; kids from places that I had seen only on television—rough-and-tumble neighborhoods where potholed streets were their only playground, where their mentors were gang leaders, and where a switchblade showing its head above a belt was saying, "I'm tougher than you! Don't mess with me." When asked about their parents, the usual answer was a grunt accompanied by a sarcastic laugh.

These kids were a mix of ethnicities. Many of them were bright, quick, and easily bored. They were potential leaders for the future—but without the opportunities that would have allowed them to grow in the right direction. And while trying to survive, many of them had made bad decisions.

Most of them had never had a job, unless you call selling drugs or sex on the nearest street corner a job. Many lived under bridges or in the backseat of a car with a single parent and several siblings. For almost all of them, life was a day-to-day struggle. All of them were proud. Many were loud. A few were afraid.

The Pathways program was designed to find the brightest of these kids and help them get through the teen years so they could make a success of their lives. One aspect of the program involved the kids going on a mission trip organized by Maranatha Volunteers International. These trips were designed to get the teens completely out of their comfort zones in a jungle or desert, where they could in effect start all over again.

The leaders had eight days to introduce the kids to another world than the one they had known—to provide experiences that would forever change the way they thought, how they approached problems, how they handled relationships, and what they did with discouragement and failure. The primary goal was to broaden their perspectives so they could make better decisions about their lives and their futures than they were making now. These trips were an instant success. Some of the kids actually changed their names as they got onto the plane so that they could really start over.

When I heard about the trips, I wished there had been a Pathways program when I was a teenager. I immediately began dreaming about how much fun working with this program could be. So, when David Lopez, Pathways coordinator for Maranatha, called me and asked if I would be willing to come along on a trip as the Pathways construction superintendent, I felt like I had gotten the best Christmas gift ever!

I came from a different world than the Pathways kids did. I had grown up in small-town Nebraska, where my mentors were my parents and the men who worked for my father building houses. But my family was poor too. I didn't get to play sports after school like most of my friends did. Instead, my dad would bring me to the site of whatever he was building at the time and I'd have to clean it up. During my teen years, I made some very poor decisions. My experiences from that part of my life gave me some insight into the Pathways kids.

Each Pathways trip was far more dangerous than any *Survivor* episode. We were dealing with kids, real kids, great kids, our country's future leaders! For instance, start with what should have been a simple challenge: getting on the plane.

Attempting to keep the group together in airports was like herding ostriches. Some would be in a bathroom, getting their last smoke. Others would be trying to use a fake ID at a bar, and still others would be picking fights at the gate. If we hadn't been there to collect them, they would simply have wandered off and gotten lost in the strange world of the airport.

Our job wasn't over when we'd gotten all twenty-five through the door and into their assigned seats. We couldn't rest or drop our guard. Most of these kids had never seen earth from anything higher than a sixteen-story building, and now they were staring out the window from thirty-five thousand feet, watching as America slowly drifted past. Most of them were afraid, and that was dangerous—so I spent a lot of time sitting beside them and listening to scary tales of the past and dreams for the future. I prayed much and often, asking God to give me the right words and spirit to work with the kids.

We learned right away that lectures and sermons were meaningless to them. The only thing that worked was getting right in there with them and working beside them on some project. Most of them had never learned how to work, so we started there, using the "teaching by doing" approach. I've helped scores of kids learn how to hold a trowel, how to lay bricks, how to mix cement, how to wash lettuce, and a thousand other simple tasks.

One fellow refused to be taught—and refused to work. He would go to his assigned place on the wall we were building and then lie down on the scaffold, making the other kids scramble over him to get their work done. He just would not work.

"Do you think you can do the job lying down like that?" I asked him.

"Yep."

"Do you think you can keep up with Shane [the leader] when you're lying down?"

"Sure. Doesn't matter."

"Couldn't you do your job more easily if you'd get up?"

"Nope. This is just right."

So we just let him wallow like that all day long. All the others were working at a really fast pace, and he was malingering.

I think he was paying attention though, because the next day, he said, "I want a different job."

That worried me, but I asked anyway: "What would you like to do?"

"I want to push the wheelbarrow."

The area where we were working was very hilly, and the job he said he wanted was the most physically demanding of all the jobs on that project.

"Have at it!" I said.

Well, that guy *ran* with the wheelbarrow, and for the rest of the trip he was a focused and motivated team member. And when we came home, he went to a recruiting station and joined the Marines.

The point is that we are in a real live war, a struggle between good and evil that, unfortunately, evil often wins. Maybe that's because evil offers things that seem cool, attractive—things that we think will make other people like us more or that promise an easy escape from our problems.

Everything that good offers is better in every way, but it's not marketed as well. Good's stuff often comes across as uninteresting, boring, irrelevant, or something for later; something we may want when we're really old. My job with the Pathways kids was to make good so interesting that they would really want it, and to help them believe that evil doesn't have to win in their lives. They *can* change. When we invite Christ to take control of our lives, He transforms us from the inside out, and good overwhelms evil!

I soon found that the best way to market the good is to choose to let Christ live the good life in me. I remake that choice every morning, and several times during the day, especially when something happens that makes me want to lash out or treat someone poorly. Many of these kids had never seen compassion or patience, and gentleness wasn't even part of their vocabulary! I determined to help them decide to make choosing the good the most important of all the choices they have to make.

I loved those kids, and I wanted them to know it. When they were "home," they didn't know what was going to happen to them next. They didn't know if they'd live through the day. They didn't know whether they'd spend most of their lives in jail. They *did* know that they couldn't change their environment, except—perhaps, by coming on a Pathways trip with Maranatha.

The bigger picture for these kids is that they needed somebody to love them, somebody to value them, appreciate them, and treat them as real people. Most of the Pathways kids had never had anyone treat them that way. This gave Dina and me a wonderful opportunity to model the good. They didn't need to know anything about the things we had done or hadn't done; all they needed to know was that we loved them. They have to know that we care, genuinely care.

Dina and I had the privilege of helping lead three trips with the Pathways kids, building schools and churches in Bagua Grande, Peru; La Libertad, Ecuador; and El Quisco, Chile. In El Quisco, we saw God and the devil in a fistfight. That port city, with its saloons lining dimly lit streets that stretch toward dark mountains, is known to be a dangerous place. Three days' leave there is near the top of every rowdy sailor's list of dreams. After weeks at sea, El Quisco translates as "Party Hard," and since the sailors will be back on their ships a day or two after their partying, there's little incentive for them to limit the mayhem they do. And sailors are only part of the challenge. El Quisco has developed an active drug culture, and that means street gangs and random killings.

While we knew that El Quisco could be a dangerous place, we felt safe because our base camp was in a section of town that was surrounded by an eight-foot-tall chain-link fence topped by many strands of barbed wire. We had come to build a school—to make life better for at least four hundred children of El Quisco.

David had arranged for a local *vaquero* to take our kids horseback riding, so the first Saturday afternoon, we boarded a beat-up school bus and bounced down to the beach to ride *caballos en la arena*. Most of our Pathways kids had never touched a real horse, much less ridden one. You can only imagine the Spanish and English confusion as Ismael el Vaquero tried to get skittish kids on confused horses. As one of the locals said, "The circus has come to town!"

We rode the beach for miles, the kids quickly finding their stride, standing in the stirrups and telling Ismael they were going to ride to Panama. Everyone rode and rode and laughed and laughed and took pictures of everyone else and the horses and posing with their horse and Ismael. It was the best possible way to start a Pathways adventure!

However, someone noticed all the cameras and followed us home to our "secure" compound. Sunday evening, while we were busily devouring supper, intruders climbed the fence and broke into several of our rooms. Even though our room was only fifty feet from where we were eating, they broke the door to our room and stole Dina's suitcase of clothes and our cameras. Then they went next door and broke into David and Alisa's room, from which they took more cameras, a computer, and some of Alisa's clothes.

We'd been robbed!

We were shocked and angry, but more shaken by the realization that even worse things could have happened. Dina had wanted to return to the room to take a shower during supper. In fact, three different times she had gotten up to leave and then sat down again. The thought made my heart weak! If Dina been in the shower or had met the thieves in the room, we could have lost far more than cameras and clothes. But something had impressed her to wait. Our angels had been at work again!

I called the police and they arrived just about sundown. One of the cops climbed the fence and peered over it at the no man's land on the other side. He slid back down and said, with an emphatic curse, "This is a very dangerous place!" Then they all went back to the station to file a report.

Looking through the fence, we could see where the thieves had come and gone on horseback, so David and I decided to deputize each other. It would take quite a hike, but if it would mean we could get our cameras, computer, and clothes back, we were certainly up for it.

We followed hoof prints in the sand for more than two hours before hitting pay dirt. The tracks showed that the thieves had dismounted and begun walking. Now we were following hoof prints, footprints, and two long lines made by the wheels on the suitcases of clothes. They screamed, "FOLLOW ME."

We followed for another fifteen minutes or so, and the tracks led us to a house in which all the lights were on even though it was 4:00 A.M. We looked at each other and decided that we needed some help.

Rather than walking back to our housing via the beach, we took to the city streets. Though we had walked much farther as we followed the tracks in the sand, we found that the suspect house was less than a mile from our camp.

We didn't have to call the police. They were waiting for us.

"Where have you been?" they asked. "We were worried about you."

"We've been out looking for our stuff—and we found it," we answered, eager to tell our story.

"That area you went into is much too dangerous for us to enter at night," the police said. "We were afraid to go out there and find you."

We almost laughed because they had guns and we had only our shorts and tennis shoes.

"Let us take you to the house where our suitcases are," we said, realizing that our stolen possessions were in more trouble than we had expected.

"Our citizens have rights too," they replied. "We can't go into a house without a warrant. That wouldn't be legal. We can't go with you."

That's when we realized we would never see our cameras again. We went to bed for about an hour and then got up and went to work, and we never heard from the cops again.

The best part of the story is how the kids reacted. I expected that they might laugh, or dash off to clobber the thieves, or demand to go home. Instead, kids who had saved up and bought small cameras or who had been allowed to take their families' cameras—a precious item for poor families—came up to us and unselfishly offered to let us use their cameras. Suddenly, we were looking at how to use ancient Instamatics and small pocket rockets that had lenses like the bottom of a Coke bottle. I was blown away by the generosity of these kids, so willing to share something they'd been eager to use themselves!

"Aren't you upset?" one of the guys asked me.

"No, not really," I was able to respond. "It was just stuff. You can always replace stuff."

That was when I realized that God wanted me to have a better camera!

God must have known that we would need someone very special to help us feel safe on this trip; another leader who understood the kids and yet had grown up—at least a bit!

Tony wasn't an ordinary guy. He was a Special Forces soldier, so successful that he had even been chosen to serve as a presidential guard. Since Tony was trained in security, he immediately took over the job of making sure our camp was safe and that no more horsemen would be able to break in. "I can take care of this, guys," Tony said, and then he went to work.

When we returned from the school building site that evening, we were greeted with floodlights that completely illuminated our perimeter. Now, there are lights, and there are lights. These were not just simple, normal, common floodlights. These were Tony's powerfully BRIGHT lights—lights like what you'd use at a military base in Afghanistan.

Tony was amazing.

Late that night, "unknowns" began firing large caliber handguns in the no-man's-land just beyond our lights. The feeling of safety the lights had brought fled in the face of reality. The houses we were living in had paper-thin walls and couldn't have slowed a rock thrown at them.

Once again the police came to visit, but this time they arrived in a pickup truck that had a spotlight and machine gun mounted on top. They drove half-heartedly into the no-man's-land, but to their relief, discovered only darkness. Many more shots were fired during our stay there, mostly after our crew was asleep at night. But no bullets came into our compound, and no one was hurt. It became obvious to all, even the cops, that we had Someone even better than Tony watching over us.

Whenever possible, we would take our Pathways kids to visit a local orphanage, or take them to other parts of the community that would help them realize how very fortunate they were. Hugging skinny orphan children brought out the best in our kids. Often they began conniving, thinking up ways to share their food, to cover kids dressed in rags with the T-shirts they were wearing, or to bring one of the kids home with them.

Both Dina and I loved everything about our Pathways adventures, but the parts that stand out most for us are the moments when we saw a disadvantaged

American kid reaching out to a stranger with unrestrained love. We were watching trustworthy leaders being born.

One remark that I will never forget came from a long-haired, skinny kid from New Jersey. He said, "I've lived four years under a bridge and four years in the back of a car, but after what I've seen today, I will never complain again."

Yes, he "got it."

Many of our Pathways kids had great leadership skills, mostly undiscovered. While building scaffolds, hauling blocks, mixing mortar, and raising walls, we formed a great team. Each ragtag team would quickly become an amazing machine, an effective construction crew. By the end of our trip, we had all been part of constructing something far more important than the building we had put up. We had built relationships. We had built trust. We had built friendships. And we saw each teenager grow into a young adult who was learning to soar like the eagle he or she was meant to be.

It's been several years since insurance requirements brought an end to the Pathways trips, but we're still in contact with many of "our kids." It's been awesome to follow them as they have chosen to live lives of service. At least three have become missionaries, and others are scientists, doctors, military leaders, teachers, and corpsmen. All began to grow and bloom after just a loving nudge in the right direction.

Sometimes a nudge is just what we need.

CHAPTER 14

Christine, the T-Shirt Girl

"Life is the first gift, love is the second, and understanding the third."

—Marge Piercy

It was really hard to build connections with some of the Pathways kids. On one trip, the team included a girl who wore the most revealing and suggestive T-shirts I'd ever seen: "Squeeze These," "Ride This," and far worse.

We hadn't sent out any T-shirt rules that year, so we left the slogans alone and just tried to connect with the girl.

No luck. She seemed to be a nice kid, but was also a hard kid with an exterior that effectively locked us out. All I was able to learn was that the police had caught her making a living as a prostitute. Other than that bit of knowledge, I had learned nothing, except that her name was Christine.

At the end of the trip, all of the kids came to us with hugs and many thank yous. Not Christine. She got off the plane and walked through security at the airport as if she didn't know any of us. And she kept right on walking. I felt terrible, as if I had completely failed her.

After all of the other kids had left, I looked out toward the main road and saw Christine. She was walking directly toward Dina and me, still wearing one of those crummy T-shirts. She found us, gave us big hugs, said Goodbye, and then she walked back through the airport and off into the crowds.

Christine's simple goodbye and the walk she made over to us to say that goodbye was our highlight for that trip. Maybe our acceptance of her had made a small dent in her armor after all!

CHAPTER 15

A Villa Near the Sea

"Don't be afraid your life will end; be afraid it will never begin."

—Grace Hansen

The public school teachers were striking for higher wages when our Pathways Mission project team arrived in Guayaquil, Ecuador, about two hours south of La Libertad, the town where we were to do our building. All the main roads were blocked with piles of burning tires, and every other road was also barricaded. We knew we were facing a serious problem. We had to drive up one of those barricaded roads—there simply was no another way to get to La Libertad!

We prayed, and then we made a phone call to the office of the governor of the province, asking for help.

He responded immediately. "If the roads are still blocked when you need to travel tomorrow morning, I will transport your group to La Libertad on my military helicopters."

We were all excited about the promised "really cool" helicopter ride when we got a message saying that the roads had been cleared. I wasn't the only disappointed person that day. All of us—other than Dina—were eager to ride in the choppers. Instead, we climbed into buses and set off for La Libertad.

Our vehicles were the first to venture onto the main road, and we found that there were still burning tires on the road. The smoke and acrid smell made our eyes water and burned our throats. We drove slowly, negotiating our way through the remaining barricades and trying to avoid looking at the blackened, smashed carcasses of the vehicles that had attempted to take this road earlier.

Eventually, we arrived at a little hotel that was one of the most enjoyable places we've ever stayed in. Our rooms looked out over the ocean, and we immediately fell in love with the owner, a stocky little Italian man who did almost everything himself, including making a huge breakfast for us every morning. He baked at least four different kinds of bread and rolls every day, all ready to eat by 6:00 A.M.

And the dinners he served each evening were absolutely gourmet quality meals, each making us look forward to the next. None of us had any idea when he found time for sleep. Maybe he went to bed and slept for a week after we left.

Minutes after we arrived at the Hotel Genova, there was a knock at our door. "We have a major problem," announced Wayne and Dayne, two of the Pathways kids. "We don't have a TV in our room."

"Don't feel bad," was my reply. "Our room doesn't have one either."

That brought peals of laughter from everyone around us. We wouldn't be using cell phones or TVs for a while.

We worked really hard during the day (we built a steel-and-concrete-block school with an auditorium that would seat four hundred students), and our evenings consisted of all of us piling into the back of a very old compact pickup and going to the *malecón* by the ocean or even better, to the local orphanage, where I overheard one of our kids say, "I will never complain again." I wrote a memo to myself when we left: "We must return to the Hotel Genova sometime soon, and bring our whole family to enjoy the pleasant company and gourmet food of the transplanted Italian who now lives in La Libertad, Ecuador."

Antonio, I learned, built the entire hotel with only one helper. It's a beautiful, three-story building with hundreds of feet of curved walls, all completed with well above-average craftsmanship. Antonio is just one of the many amazing people whom we've had the pleasure of meeting in our wanderings, and he is certainly the best cook we've found anywhere.

Dayne went home after this trip and went straight to the top of his class in the military academy he went to. Wayne also grew into a fantastic young man. We keep in touch by Facebook and phone. He called me one day when I was standing in a cancer treatment center in Houston, Texas. He wanted to know how he could become a Maranatha employee. "I loved what we did that week, Mr. Terry," he said. "I want to do it full time."

Wayne's life has never been the same since that trip. Instead, it's been better.

I can SO relate.

CHAPTER 16

Two Angels in the Alley

*"Vision is the world's most desperate need. There are no hopeless situations,
only people who think hopelessly."*

—Winifred Newman

We landed in the New York–size metropolis of Lima, Peru, boarded a bus, and headed far away from civilization into the Andes Mountains. Eight hours later, after bouncing over some very unkempt roads, we found our destination: Bagua Grande, *"Corazón de Amazonas."*

Bagua Grande is a mining town roughly fifty thousand strong, high in the mountains and far off the tourist maps. Our job was to build a school in Bagua Grande.

It seemed like the entire town was waiting for us and eager to treat us as celebrities. A TV news team documented our daily progress and interviewed anyone who would stand in front of the camera and talk to them. Why were we such celebrities? Because we came in colors they had never seen before. Our Pathways kids were made up of African Americans, Asians, Caucasians, and Hispanics. We were colored like a box of crayons they had never even imagined! The people cheered when we drove down the street, and they were anxious to touch our skin to see what difference there might be.

We stayed in a small hotel that may have never had a tourist as an overnight guest, and we were told that we were the only visitors in the entire town. Our hotel rooms had a bed, a toilet without a seat, and a shower without much water—if you waited long enough, it might give you a few drops every now and then. When you were lucky enough to get a trickle of water, you had to soap and rinse quickly, because if the people in the room next door turned on their shower, the water went away and left you all soaped up.

One morning I was determined to get a decent shower, so I set my alarm for 3:45 A.M. When the alarm rang, I got into the shower, turned the handles, and was thoroughly disappointed when not even one drop came out of the shower head.

Frustrated, I wrapped myself in a towel and tromped out to the front desk. After a few taps on the small silver bell, a head popped up followed by a body. The man wanted to know what I might possibly want at that time of the morning. My Spanish is *muy malo,* and he spoke not a word of English. Fortunately, my towel told the story. We walked to the roof together and found that the concrete water tank was empty. The little water that was dribbling into it was being called for before the drops hit the bottom of the tank.

I went back to the room, put on some work clothes, and thirty minutes later discovered that one of the hotel toilets had a bad flapper. Once that was fixed, I had to wait another forty-five minutes for enough water to accumulate for me to take a shower. Then the water was cold, just as it was every other morning, but at least it was water! And since the temperature, even at 5:00 A.M., was already in the nineties, we didn't mind the cold water one bit.

What was the most disturbing thing about our digs? Every wall in our room had at least two thousand cockroaches on it at any one time. We unzipped our suitcases just long enough to get what we wanted, and when we got home, we unpacked a long way from the house. The accommodations were really bad, but when you go to a town that never sees tourists, that's what you get.

Every night the town kids came to play soccer with us on the narrow, brick-paved street outside our hotel. It was us against them, and there were always some *pesos* on the line. Not many *pesos,* as the town kids had to pool their coins to have enough to amount to anything. They did manage to kick our butts every night, but not without a good struggle. I think we expended as much energy in two hours of playing soccer as we had expended at work all day!

The building we were constructing was a difficult one. The concrete blocks weighed about twenty pounds each; we had to mix the mortar mixed by hand; and we were laboring under a scorching sun without a cloud in sight. The building was about one hundred feet square, and some walls extended twenty or more feet into the air. The first few days must have shown our Pathways team what hell will be like—at least temperature-wise. But we slowly became acclimated to the weather, drank lots of water, and used lots of sunscreen. The experience we were sharing also morphed us into a team.

Please keep in mind that the kids we were working with were from the poorer, more violent parts of big cities. We were as far from what they were used to as we could be. Most often, this is where the magic of mission trips happens.

Nicknames helped keep us laughing. On this trip, we had The Bishop and Prince Edward—two young men who were assigned the job of managing the building of a large section of one wall. I watched them dig deep when their helpers were fading, keeping on even though they were as tired as their cohorts.

I had the easy job: making sure that the school building was built correctly.

David, our fearless leader, had far greater challenges. I doubt that he got much sleep on that trip, as the kids were either trying to shack up or sneak out to the bar and party when they were supposed to be in bed. David also spent his share of time in the hot sun, helping to direct the construction. My hat is still off to him for doing such a great job of leading on these trips, but my guess is that returning back to work at the Maranatha office felt a little like heaven for him.

One of our rules that we emphasized most was "Never walk alone in the town. It isn't safe." Our dining hall was only a five-block walk from the hotel, but the route ran through areas that were narrow and dark.

One morning Dina began to feel ill as she was helping prepare breakfast. Disregarding our rule and all advice, she walked alone from the mess hall toward the hotel. About a block into her walk, two scruffy men in worn-out jeans turned into the alley she was following and walked straight toward her. Instead of walking on by when they passed her, they turned around and began following her. Dina began to walk faster, and so did they. Every step was raising Dina's heart- and prayer-rates.

Just as they were catching up with her, a woman with a small child appeared in the middle of the street, just standing there and watching. Dina didn't see her walk into the street, and she certainly hadn't come up from behind. She just showed up. When she did, the two men made an abrupt right turn and disappeared. Dina waved at the woman and walked the rest of the way to the hotel alone.

Or was she?

Do you think angels can take on the appearance of a woman and a little girl? We do.

CHAPTER 17

Christianity Evolves in the Galapagos Islands

"You never know what good things will pour in when the heart is open to life."

—Unknown

When you walk down Charles Darwin Street, walk on the beach side of the street, but be sure to cross the street road before you get to the Seventh-day Adventist church. They're a crazy cult, and you'll be safer if you stay away from them."

Everyone in the fishing and tourism town of Puerto Ayora in the Galapagos Islands knew this was true, and for years they all walked on the other side of the street when they passed the Adventist church. In fact, the feelings were so strong that when the Adventists held public meetings in a theater, the leader of another church in the town promised to excommunicate any of his members who attended them.

When Miguel Gallardo heard the ultimatum, he laughed. "I had been invited to the meetings," he says, "but I had no interest in going. I worked at the Darwin Center and was a member of another church. Then their projector broke down, and they asked me to repair it. I didn't know anything about repairing projectors, but I repaired it anyway! Then they asked me to go to the meeting to be sure the projector stayed working. I liked what I heard and stayed for the full series. My family and three others became Adventists that month, and we decided to change the way people felt about the church."

That's when they started a school. Eighteen students came at first, then twenty-four, and then thirty—all the students and their parents telling everyone in Puerto Ayora about the excellent teachers, the good values, and the fine education at "Colegio Loma Linda."

"People began walking on our side of the street," one of the graduates says, "begging the principal to let their children attend."

In 2007, the school, which was named after the marine biological field station that Loma Linda University operated on the property for a few years, had 276 students crammed into a jerry-rigged cluster of multiuse buildings.

"The facilities are inadequate, but the teachers are the best on the islands," said the local director of education and culture. "Parents send their children here because they want them to have values like the Adventist professors." Then he added, "We are all very proud of this school, but the facilities do need help."

This is where we came in. Maranatha called and asked if Dina and I would join one of the Galapagos volunteer trips to help supervise construction of a new school.

"You bet!" I answered.

We are proud to have been two of the more than 350 Maranatha volunteers who came in four different teams to dig ditches, build forms, pour concrete, lay block, paint walls, teach English, pull teeth, and cook giant pots of beans and rice on Santa Cruz island. The old school on Charles Darwin Street was transformed into a secondary school, and the primary students moved into a brand-new campus up the hill.

"I can't imagine why anyone would go on a normal vacation when a person can do this," Steve Fisher, one of the January volunteers told me. "We're helping to make a difference everywhere on the Galapagos."

Each of the four volunteer projects included a six-island cruise on the *Galapagos Legend*. "There aren't enough digital memory cards in the world to hold all of the pictures this crew is taking," said Luis, one of the Galapagos National Park guides.

Luis was probably right, as all of us clicked away unceasingly at iguanas, sea lions, frigate birds, swallowtail gulls, albatross chicks, lizards, mockingbirds, yellow warblers, and the favorite . . . blue-footed boobies.

Some of my favorite Galapagos pictures are of those birds. They were the most fun, with their black-and-white tuxedos and brilliant blue feet! There were also some amazing flowers and the yellow land iguanas that looked like dinosaurs. What impressed me the most, though, was the general feeling of tranquility that pervaded the islands—as if human beings and nature meshed a little bit better there than in most other places on earth.

On our working trip to the Galapagos Islands, it was easy to get carried away with the animals, birds, and Sally Lightfoot crabs, but the project was fantastic too. It's special to go to an island where you know you can't live unless you were born there. The *Galapagueñas* could probably move up the economic scale a bit if they went elsewhere, but most of them don't. That's wild!

We had huge challenges on the job. In fact, there were days when I doubted we were going to get it done. Then all of a sudden, as if in direct answer to prayer, God resolved each problem.

For example, we had to find a bulldozer and enough dirt to fill the back two-thirds of the land where we were building the new school. There was no way we could get both the school building and the required outbuildings on the flat section of the lot near the road. We had to be able to build on the rest of the land too.

That seemed impossible. The fill dirt had to come from the other side of the island, and all four of the dump trucks on the island were busy. And the only bulldozer

A Galapagos iguana—remember, "beauty is in the eye of the beholder."

Maybe you prefer this sea lion pup?

was working way over on the other side and wasn't available in time to meet our need.

Then, boom—trucks started dumping loads of dirt on the land, and Sunday morning, when everyone knew it was "impossible" to get the dozer, the muddy yellow Cat came rattling up on the flatbed of a large red truck. It took the operator from sunrise to sunset to get the job done, but he did it—happily!

No, that's not really true. God did it.

Each evening, after our work crews disbanded and we sent everyone back for supper, six or seven of us piled into an ancient Toyota taxi and bounced over the broken roads to the fishing dock to watch "the best show on the islands," a pitched battle among frigates, pelicans, sea lions, and fishermen. There's lots of showing off, laughter, and begging going on—all to the accompaniment of digital cameras clicking voraciously. Those evenings provided another great memory from the Galapagos. Fishy smells, dangerous beaks, and great pictures!

Dina and I worked on the Galapagos school project for several weeks. It was *hot,* but we enjoyed sweating together with about eighty-five other volunteers. It was like being in an all-day sauna—with pelicans!

Several of my favorite pictures come from a tiny island several hours and boat-bounces away from Puerto Ayora. I had to bargain hard with the boat owner, but we finally came to an agreement we could both live with. All I wanted to do was photograph a red-footed booby, and they say this little rocky outcrop is the only place where you can see them. There are blue-footed boobies on several of the islands, but the red-foots have been banished to this one rock. That I had to see!

The boat was large enough for a dozen people, so I gathered friends and set off booby-hunting, with Dina's permission. The weather was perfect when we started out. (Have you heard this story before?) Then it turned gray and ugly, and motion sickness engulfed most of us.

It felt like it took us three days to get to Punta Pitt, and then the captain wanted to slip past the island and anchor in a little bay nearby.

"Can we see the red-footed boobies from the bay?"

"Well, no. But it's safer there."

"Then not yet! We came out here to see red-footed boobies!"

So we did, though it was a miracle none of us fell overboard trying to hold long lenses steady while the captain was trying to keep the boat on the water rather than on the rocks. We did get our pictures, and yes, there are red-footed boobies on that little outcrop. I wonder what they did to be banished way out there, away from their cousins.

We finally let the captain have his way and anchor the boat in a green bay of Punta Pitt. Wow, what a place! You know how, when you post a really special photo on Facebook, people respond as if they're inarticulate and monosyllabic? They just say something like, "Wow!" Sometimes that's the only thing you can say. When I look back at my Galapagos pictures and come to the ones I took that afternoon at Punta Pitt, about all I can say is, "Wow!"

You would have loved the turtles in the bay! There were dozens and dozens of them, making love in the surf, chasing seals, and celebrating their future.

Then the storm blew in, and the ride home was forgettable.

Back to our construction project. As I said earlier, there were so many unexpected solutions to problems we faced on that project that I have no question about who was in charge. This was truly God's school.

I was awed by that fact one afternoon when Esmeralda, the principal of Colegio Loma Linda, told us about Enrique.

She said, "Yesterday something amazing happened. We had some parents who wanted to try to get their son Enrique on the right track morally, but when they talked about sending him to our school, the Mother Superior for their district, along with several of the boy's aunties, warned against it. Enrique's parents sent him anyway, and he became one of our favorite students. Then, a few weeks ago, they had to take him out of school because of finances."

Principal Esmeralda knows and loves each student personally. Watch her at school, and you'll see a lifelong mother at work. Listen as she counsels parents, and you'll hear the heart of a pastor. Ask parents about her work, and they'll shower her with praise. When Esmeralda got to this point in Enrique's story, she paused and wiped her eyes before she could continue.

"This is so amazing and wonderful! Yesterday, Enrique's parents brought him back to school, saying that all the aunties had demanded that he return to Loma Linda. And the Mother Superior who had discouraged his attendance is paying his tuition!"

Everything has changed for the children of Santa Cruz. Now people cross the street to bring their children to school, to attend graduation, and to participate in the religious services there. People's opinion of Seventh-day Adventists has evolved from them being considered a crazy cult, to being essential to the social fabric of the islands.

Because of the vision and generosity of the Maranatha Galapagos volunteers, the project in Puerto Ayora grew from building a six-classroom school building to developing a school campus with thirteen classrooms plus space for a new library, a state-of-the-art computer center, and a science laboratory. The volunteers saw the need, realized what a better school could do, and began drawing plans on napkins and concrete forms. The result is a divine victory.

"The Adventists have taught us all so much about values," the director of education and culture says. "They have given us a model of quality and love that has brought us together and made our community better."

Miguel Gallardo, one of the church leaders, says, "It's a miracle that Maranatha brought people from around the world to come to our town and help us serve our people better. The masons, the cement workers, the painters, they come from so many religions and from so many parts of the world, yet they are like family with us. With them, we are able to do God's miracles as one. This is a fulfillment of all my dreams for our islands."

CHAPTER 18

Ninety-Nine Miles

"The World is a book, and those who do not travel read only a page."

—Saint Augustine

My bucket list has long included two unlikely items: visiting Cuba while it is a communist regime, and piloting a military jet aircraft. Jets were just coming of age when I was a youngster, and my first ambition in life was to be a fighter pilot. To be at forty thousand feet, punching holes in the atmosphere, seemed like the perfect job. But when I was in seventh grade, I had to get glasses to see distant things clearly, and I realized then that I would never fly a jet.

The Cuba dream did materialize though! In 2007, my youngest daughter, Terra, and I were invited to attend a church dedication in Camaguey, Cuba. Once again, we would be traveling with Maranatha, our favorite nonprofit organization, but this would be an unusual trip for me, as we weren't going to plan something or build something, but simply to dedicate a church.

Maranatha has had a tremendous impact on the island of Cuba, remodeling more than two hundred churches, building a seminary, and as far as possible, meeting some of the needs of the Cuban people. The Cuban government pays close attention to what religious groups do in the country, but it has given the Seventh-day Adventist Church considerable support. The country leaders often affirm church members for helping guide the moral development of the nation.

We arrived in Havana in the middle of the afternoon after a short flight from Cancun, Mexico. Secured away in my carry-on luggage was a letter from the United States Department of State, with their official seal, granting us permission to travel to Cuba for humanitarian service. I have guarded that letter carefully over the years, especially since I heard that I was required to be able to produce it at any time within seven years of visiting the island or face a million-dollar fine!

Havana International Airport rates number one for the number and intensity of security checks one must go through before entering the country. They certainly

The cars on the streets of Havana suggest you've been transported back into the 1950s.

want our dollars, but are vigilant regarding smuggled goods. The third security check was the most thorough. The security guard transformed the contents of our suitcases from neatly pressed and folded clothing into tightly wadded balls. Dina had sent with us four sealed envelopes for Terra to read; one per day. For some reason, the security guard didn't open the envelopes, but tore them into small squares. It made for a crazy memory and jigsaw-puzzle challenge every night.

The hotel was nice, a Hilton hotel that the government had transformed first into offices and now into a pleasant tourist hotel. Perhaps eighteen or twenty stories high, it's a beautiful structure with lots of granite and glass. We were greeted by some of the most overqualified bellmen ever—doctors, lawyers, and other professionals who were augmenting their meager incomes by working a second job. I would guess that they made more in tips than they made in their primary jobs. In 2007, a doctor with one specialty made US$25 per month. In 2012, that same doctor, with three specialties now, made US$22.

We were greeted at the elevator door by a machine-gun-carrying guard. He made sure no locals entered the elevator; they weren't allowed above the lobby as it was against the law for a Cuban citizen to stay in a hotel. The government didn't want the locals to watch CNN or any other news source that might provide a view of the world that didn't meet their approval. Radio, television, billboards, and the Internet are tightly controlled in Cuba. And images of Che Guevara and Castro abound. Going to Cuba is like stepping into another dimension. One of my first impressions: Cuba has a feel like that of Hanoi, where it pays to walk softly and cast a small shadow—unless you drive a gleaming, black government Mercedes.

Our very nice eighth-floor room pleasantly surprised us. It overlooked Havana, providing a clear view of the Malecón and the distant citadel of El Morro. An old but working TV set, one of the very few portals to the world, sat in the corner of the room. How ironic that it was provided for people like me, but not for our hotel maid or almost anyone else in the city! The bath, with its granite floor, walls, and ceiling, was fit for a palace. The bed was adequate, the sheets coarse, the bedspread aged and thin. We called the front desk asking for an extra blanket, and in a few minutes a maid arrived with a small armload of tablecloths.

In the best Spanish we could muster, we again asked for a blanket, and again she offered the tablecloths. "Take as many as you want," she said.

Still not buying in, and knowing that there were at least eight floors above us that were unoccupied (no lights were on), I asked if there were other rooms in the hotel that might have a blanket we could use.

"No," she replied. "If you would like these, you can have them. There are no other blankets in the hotel."

We took several.

The hotel situation in Cuba is interesting, to say the least. Foreign investors who choose to do business there purchase a hotel and then cede half ownership to the government. If they make any major missteps, they lose their stake and the government takes all. Until very recently, hotels like ours were exclusively for tourists, and at close to US$300 per night, they still are.

The breakfast buffet was a feast: fruits of every kind, more than two dozen different breads, five flavors of milk, cooks at our command to create anything we could imagine that started with eggs. The menu was longer than those at almost any restaurant in Nebraska. The hard thing to stomach was that the very people who were serving us were hungry, too poor to feed their families, and prohibited from eating any of the food they were serving us. Up to 90 percent of Cuba's "wealth" goes to tourism rather than to meeting the needs of Cubans.

The next day we were bussed to the airport and ushered onto the tarmac where a thirty-two-passenger, Soviet-built Yak-40 was waiting for us. The paint was old, but a quick glance revealed adequate tires, no visible leaks, and an eager crew. This plane loaded from the rear, and most of our group chose seats close to the door. The aluminum tag on the fuselage door was stamped "Manufactured in 1968."

Terra and I walked toward the mostly empty front of the cabin. We had no trouble choosing which side to sit on. All the windows on the left side were crazed to the point of being obscure, but the windows on the right side had new, clear glass. So, we sat on the right, hoping for a good view of the Cuban countryside.

When I sat down, the back of the seat collapsed, its latch broken. The seat belt? Only half was there.

"Is this a problem?" I asked the flight attendant who was standing at the front of the plane.

"Don't worry. You will be fine," she replied.

She was holding a basket of hard candy, which we quickly learned was to be our beverage, snack, and dessert all wrapped in one. I took a moment to admire the high-tech, neatly fitted piece of three-eighths-inch plywood that served as the cockpit door. There was a miniscule latch on the door and a lock that looked like it had come from a bubble gum vending machine.

"I used to be a pilot," I told the flight attendant. "May I look in the cockpit?"

"Why certainly," she replied. "Let's just wait until we take off."

The Yak-40 is a three-engine jet, so when we rolled onto the runway, it didn't take long to hit V_1. As the pilot rotated the aircraft into a steep climb, the attendant struggled to stand and make her way to the cockpit door. Reaching into her apron, she produced a key for the door. Then, walking uphill into the cockpit, she motioned for me to follow. Surprised, but not waiting for her to change her mind, I followed her up the steep aisle.

The pilot's greeting was even more surprising. We were now flying at maybe four hundred feet above sea level and climbing hard. He stood up, gestured to the now-empty left seat, and said, "Please, sit down and fly." I said, "No thank you," but he was not to be turned down. Sitting back down and adjusting the throttles, he looked at the copilot and used a few motions and words I didn't understand. Then in English, he said, "This man is going to fly today," and with that the copilot got up and went back to occupy the seat I had just left beside Terra.

I sat down in the right seat, buckled in, and smiled at the captain. A big grin broke across his face and, in perfect English, he said, "Throttle back to eighty percent."

The pilot was the only one of the three flight crew members who spoke English. I heard what he said, but wondered whether he was talking to me. Yep, he was looking straight at me and expecting me to do something. My left hand found its way to the three knobs and pulled back a little. They moved pretty easily, and I found 80 percent right away!

I did a quick assessment of our navigational equipment and was more than a bit disturbed. The directional guidance system wouldn't hold a heading; the compass was dry; the radio turned off, to be used only in bursts of three minutes or less; and the transponder was on standby. The pilot then reached over and turned on the one-color radar, the only piece of original electronics that worked. Pointing at a small black box on the ceiling, the pilot said, "GPS." That one instrument was all he needed.

It was a beautiful, clear day, making it possible for us to see for miles. We climbed to twenty-four thousand feet and flew down the middle of the island in a southeast direction. Below us was a quilt-work of tobacco farms, sugar cane fields, and other agriculture.

I looked over to the left and wondered if I might be looking at the tip of Florida.

"Miami?" I asked.

"Yes," he replied.

"Do you ever think about it?"

He looked at me long and hard and then slowly fashioned his reply.

"I think about it every day, but there is something that always keeps me from considering it. There are two men at the back of this plane. Each holds a machine pistol, and each has the same assignment: to make sure this plane doesn't go to Miami. Neither of them trusts the other, so they always have their guns trained on each other just in case. However, if I shift course to Miami, one of them will kill me."

We flew in silence for several minutes as I pondered what he had told me. The captain broke the silence. "Before we begin descending, I would like you to go to the back of the plane pretending that you have to go to the bathroom. You'll see what I am talking about."

I made my way to the back of the airplane and tried not to stare at the two men the captain had described. They were in the last row, well-dressed, each in an aisle seat. Each held a machine pistol with a long banana clip and a silencer, and the gun was aimed at the other guard's head. Neither man acknowledged my approach until I was standing in front of them, waiting for them to pull their weapons back to give me enough room to pass. They pulled their weapons back for a couple of seconds and allowed me to walk to the bathroom, which was a cramped affair, all stainless steel and very noisy, especially since the jet engines were roaring just a few feet away. I returned to the two keepers of the aisle. They again raised their guns to let me pass while never acknowledging my presence in any other way. They seemed to be intent on staring each other down.

Returning to the cockpit, I waved to the copilot, who was still sitting in my seat, and then stepped back into the cockpit and dropped into his seat. As I buckled in, the captain looked at me and said, "My prayer is that one day I will hit a bump big enough that they will shoot each other." With that he reached over and pulled the throttles back, and we started our descent into Camaguey.

A moment later the captain leaned over and said, "You're going to land this airplane today."

As the airport came into view, the captain gave headings, throttle settings, and airspeeds. I don't know who was having the most fun, but was still pretty sure it was me. The VASI approach lights were now in sight, and even though they didn't work, they did tell us that we were getting close to the ground.

"It's all yours," the captain said.

"No, I don't want it to be all mine," I responded.

"Go ahead," he said. "I will watch everything." Then he patted me on the shoulder and gave the throttles a slight nudge back, and we began our flare-out over the runway. As I pulled the yoke back a little and then even further, the plane settled into its landing position. I looked at the captain and said, "Please land the plane."

He gave me the "what a wimp" look, and three seconds later we were rolling softly down the runway. To this day, I don't know whether he knew I was a pilot. He never asked, and I had never said I was. Yes, I had piloted a private plane and had flown the required minimum number of hours, but I had not kept current.

That was one of the coolest airline rides I would ever have. The only other flight that could even come close was also on Cubana Air, but that is another story.

Hundreds of church members, guests, and church dignitaries met us at the church. The celebration and dedication was a highly emotional event for the church members, many of whom had prayed and sacrificed for years to make this a reality. The building was packed to capacity and overflowing before it had even been dedicated!

Cuban churches get used much more than American churches do. There are events every evening, and the weekends are packed with meetings from Friday evening through late Saturday. Maybe having less outside distractions can be good for one's spiritual and social life, although the Cuban church members might argue that point. Almost everything about life outside the church is controlled by the government, and there are government representatives at every church meeting to make sure that they don't become political.

Dinner was served in a park nearby and consisted of a very nice arrangement of rice and beans served with thinly sliced tomatoes. It had taken several people three days to secure enough rice and beans on the black market to feed our group. Had they been apprehended without an official government receipt, each shopper could have been sentenced to ten years in jail.

People say there was a Cuban farmer who butchered his cow, and since it is against the law for a Cuban to eat beef, he gave the meat to the government. But after giving the meat away, he processed the brains and entrails for his family, and that cost him ten years in jail. Beef is only for tourists, and someone told the police about the brains.

Distrust permeates almost everything in Cuba, even large political gatherings. Each year the Cuban government holds a Million Man March to remind the people and tell the world that Cuba is stronger than America. Here's how it works: Most of the workforce works for the government, and all government employees are required to join the march. Your boss hands you a stick with a flag on the end and tells you when to be at the parade square. Failure to comply will earn you a ten-year jail sentence. And if you notice that someone is missing or even late, you can turn them in and earn up to six months' extra pay.

Sunday morning we were back in Havana, wandering through the streets of the old city. Visiting Old Havana is an unbelievable adventure—walking the cobblestone streets, admiring the fantastically ornate old buildings, watching street artists paint pictures of Cuban life, and listening to small bands play traditional music. In Cathedral Square, we saw an eighty-year-old woman who was smoking a huge cigar with a four-inch-long ash hanging off the end. It wasn't only a *Cuban* cigar, it was also the fattest, biggest, longest Cuban cigar ever made!

I couldn't believe my eyes and asked for her picture. "One dollar," she replied. For some dumb reason, I decided to try to take a picture without paying her the dollar. Not a good idea! I left without the photo, and halfway to the airport started kicking myself for not wanting to give her a buck to get what had to be the best picture of the trip! Six months later, the *National Geographic* cover featured a picture just like the one I missed that morning!

When we came to the Capitol building, I met a man taking pictures of tourists with a 1910 pinhole camera. I declined his offer for a photo and was immediately accosted by an angry mob shouting unprintable adjectives. My guide said, "If you don't want to get hurt, you should get your picture taken. He really needs the money."

I handed the cameraman a buck, and he sat me down on the Capitol steps. Putting his head under the cloth, he aligned everything and then removed the lens cap for a few seconds to expose the image. A leather apron with two pouches hung at his side, and he deftly slid the negative into the first pouch, and next, into the developing solution. Then he used broad daylight as the fixer. Somehow, he was able to make a pinhole photo that showed my face at the bottom and the Capitol at the top. He must have had the top half ready before he took my picture. An ingenious man having the time of his life harassing tourists for a living!

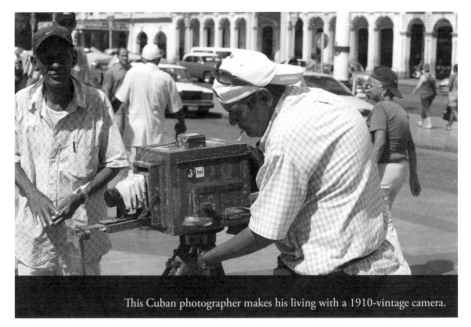

This Cuban photographer makes his living with a 1910-vintage camera.

While we were walking downtown, my attorney friend Tom needed a *baño*. We finally located one. It was not a big bathroom, but it was a clean one, as the janitor, a woman, was busy mopping the floor. Tom looked at me and said, "Really? I don't think so."

I said, "But Tom, you need a bathroom."

"I know," he groaned, "but it looks like this one is being cleaned."

The woman looked at Tom, smiled, and in Spanish said, "Please come in. Everything is fine."

Tom is bilingual, so he understood perfectly. Looking a bit perplexed, he stepped up to the urinal. That was one of the few times I have taken a picture in a bathroom. The photo pictures Tom standing at the urinal with the cleaning lady mopping around his shoes as he is using the facility! It was one of the funniest things I'd seen in a long time.

The airport bathroom had much the same arrangement. A woman sat in the men's toilet area selling toilet paper by the square. If you needed more, she would bring it to your stall.

I asked her if she charged the same price for the paper she delivered.

"Yes," she said.

She should think about it and maybe charge double.

Our bus tour of the surrounding areas was most interesting. I wish I had made an audio recording of our guide's chatter. He informed us that the American White House and the Cuban White House are identical and it's unclear who copied whom. I spoke up to set the record straight, but the guide reiterated that no one knew for sure. That was enough for me, and the conversation turned to something we could agree on.

One of the last stops was at El Morro, the old fort overlooking the bay. Built by the Spaniards in 1589, its massive gates and presence are most impressive even today. I wanted a picture of the walkway that ran up to the prison, and I wanted to take it from a little higher position as I thought the photo would be better. So, I stepped up onto a six-inch-high, cast-iron horse tether and stretched tall for the photo. Immediately, two men behind me began to shout in Spanish and dashed towards me. *Get the picture and then ask for forgiveness,* I thought. Before I could get down, there was an AK-47 barrel in my ear, and another AK-47 pointing up my nostril. Much too excitedly, the soldier whose gun was up my nose informed me that I was defacing government property and could be given six months in jail or a ten-thousand-dollar fine.

Blood was seeping from my nose, but it seemed like I was the only one who cared. I very carefully took off my shirt—which got rid of the gun barrels to my head—and began wiping the dust off of the black-painted, cast-iron post. When the soldiers saw that it was unhurt, they muttered something, one pushed me with his foot while I was still kneeling down, and then they both walked away. No one got a picture of the moment. Welcome to Cuba.

By far the best ride on the island is the ride that *leaves* it. Ours was in an aging Tu-154 airliner built in the USSR. Another plane with three big jet engines at the rear, this one was built for short takeoffs from gravel runways, so it has plenty of power. We sat near the rear of the plane, where the takeoff must feel something like a shuttle launch. The whole plane shook like a leaf in a prairie windstorm, and we climbed hard, roaring like a million angry demons. My seatmate was saying something, but I had no idea what. It was wonderfully loud! Fifteen thousand feet is the maximum altitude they trust these old birds to fly, and we reached that altitude in an amazingly short time.

My memories of Cuba? Old American cars—lots of them. Chevys, Buicks, Fords, Cadillacs, Plymouths, Packards, and more; many of them convertibles. Each car is brightly painted and has carefully polished chrome. It felt like we were on the track of a classic car show. Some of the old muscle cars have Soviet four-cylinder diesels, others have Japanese truck rear ends or other odd combinations of working parts. Most of the bodies are more Bondo than steel. The owners do whatever it takes to keep them going. One of the Cuban drivers told me, "If it is made of steel, we can make it last forever."

The Cubans are wonderful people. They didn't choose to be born on the island, and they're making the best of unfortunate conditions. They have many traits that we should have. They are industrious, generous, and kind, and they are happy and hopeful. They left me with many things to think about.

One of the most asked for items? American flag pins.

Go figure.

CHAPTER 19

Eddie and the Giraffes

"The greatest achievements are those that benefit others."

—Denis Waitley

Dina and I were pretty puckered up about having Sheree, our twenty-five-year-old girl, living in back-country Mozambique. It didn't sound very safe, so, trying to be responsible parents, we concluded that we would go to Africa and make sure that Sheree would be OK.

We decided to spend a month with her and asked her to choose two places she would like to see. She chose Zanzibar and Victoria Falls, so we headed off into Zambia and Zimbabwe to see the falls. We'd never been there and didn't know anyone on either side of the river, so everything was a new adventure.

We stayed a couple days and really enjoyed the falls. It's incredibly beautiful and has become one of our favorite places in the entire world.

The evening before we were to leave, Eddie, a very nice safari operator, befriended us. He took us out for a bush dinner and drove us around the town of Victoria Falls once more. Then he asked if he could take us to the airport in the morning. We said, "Sure," and went to bed.

That next morning, on the way to the airport, Dina found three wooden giraffes, each about three feet tall and crying out for transport to America. She bought the lot for eleven dollars, and we rushed to the airport.

"It's going to be really hard to get those giraffes home," I told Sheree. She agreed, and we began imagining solutions for giraffe immigration.

I looked at Eddie, our driver. He looked pretty responsible, so I asked him if he would mind shipping the giraffes home for me. He agreed to do it, so then I asked, "How much will it cost?"

"Oh, it won't be very much. Don't worry," Eddie answered.

So I gave him seventy-five dollars, thinking that would surely cover the shipping charge. We flew home, and months went by without any giraffes arriving at our home in Nebraska.

Dina reminded me often that she'd said the driver was "never going to send them."

I said, "You know, maybe not, but I think he will. Someday."

When they arrived, as I hoped they would, they came in a DHL truck. They were packed tightly in a very well-made wooden crate. The careful woodwork would have made my brother Bruce proud! The three giraffes maybe weighed a pound apiece, but the wooden crate weighed about thirty pounds!

I took one look at the bright yellow truck with the letters *DHL* on the side and thought, *Wow! That was expensive!*

We unpacked the giraffes and ushered them, hale and hearty and probably hungry, into our living-room zoo.

About that time, Eddie called. "Did you get your package?" he asked.

"Yes, we did. Thank you! Everything was just fine."

"I'm sorry it took so long for me to send it to you," Eddie said, "but I had to save up a little bit to get the money."

"Eddie," I asked, "what do I owe you?"

I'll never forget his answer. "Mr. Terry, I would much rather have your friendship than your money."

"But what if you could have both?" I asked.

"We won't ever talk about this again," he answered.

When I hung up, I called DHL to ask what it had cost to ship the giant wooden box from Victoria Falls to our house. "Three hundred seventy-five dollars," the DHL fellow said.

I couldn't believe it!

I called Eddie back and told him that he had to tell me how I could get him the money. He'd had to save three months' wages so he could send me the eleven dollars' worth of wooden giraffes! I couldn't believe it and was so humbled by this young man's service to Dina and me.

"Please don't send me the money," he said. "It would never get to me. But someday there may be some way you can help me. If so, I'll let you know."

We hung up again and placed the giraffes in an even more prominent—and safe—position.

Several months later, Eddie called and asked if I could find him an unlocked cell phone. They're very hard to get in Zimbabwe, and what it cost me was just about what I owed him.

So, I said, "Sure," bought one, and put it in a secure package. The packaging pushed what I was paying to about twice what I owed him, but we sent it and smiled.

The friendship strengthened.

About four months later, Eddie called again and asked if I could help him get a printer. That made me a little nervous, especially since I knew what it cost me to ship a cell phone!

"Can't you buy a printer over there?" I asked Eddie.

"Sure. But they're really old, and I'd have to pay a thousand dollars for a bad one."

So we went down to Office Depot and bought an HP printer that was an all-in-one—and more! I think there was even a button that would make Indian flat bread. All it didn't do was speak in Shona.

We filled it with ink, extra cartridges, and lots of extra paper, and fitted it into a box. And right on the very top, we put a copy of one of my favorite books, *Steps to Christ*. Then we went to the bank, withdrew all our money, and headed off to DHL. Fearfully.

The total cost was seven hundred twenty-five dollars. Far too much. But we decided that this was an investment in a relationship with Eddie and his family. An investment in which money was not to be the issue.

Several silent weeks went by. Then Eddie called.

I took a deep breath, not knowing what I might hear, and listened to Eddie's first words.

"Brother Terry, that is the most wonderful book I have ever read in all of my life! When I opened the box, I sat down and read it from cover to cover without stopping."

Eddie was born in the Zimbabwe bush, and his mother, who believed in reading as the best activity for all children, walked thirty miles each way just to get books for Eddie. Eddie learned to read by going letter-by-letter and word-by-word through the books his mother brought him. No school, just encouragement, affirmation, and more books!

When he settled down enough for me to get a word in, I asked him if he liked the printer too.

"Oh yes, Brother Terry," he said. "It is the most beautiful printer I've seen in my life!"

"How does it work?"

"I don't know. My computer isn't modern enough to operate it, but I'm fixing that over here. But I sure do love that book about Christ!"

I learned a very important message that day. My best efforts to help someone in another country may just "kill them with technology." The best I can do is share the simple truth of God's grace.

CHAPTER 20

Eddie and the School Request

"A journey is better measured in friends rather than miles."

—Tim Cahill

The next time we went to Africa, we went to build a school in Maputo, Mozambique, many miles from Victoria Falls, Zimbabwe, which is where Eddie lives. But we decided to go a few days early and visit our friend Eddie.

We had fun packing our suitcases for that trip. We filled them with things we thought Eddie and his family might need. Zimbabwe was going through a major time of hardship. They couldn't get food or clothing, so we packed to help!

That was good till we arrived in Johannesburg, South Africa, where we would be stopping just for the night, before journeying on. The customs dudes, though, demanded more than four hundred dollars for us to "import" beans and rice into their country.

When we arrived in Victoria Falls, Eddie was waiting. He helped us through immigration and customs and was so excited to see us that we thought we were going to be smothered in his hugs.

I don't know how he managed to buy enough fuel to get to the airport. Gas cost seventeen dollars a gallon, if you could find it! And Victoria Falls stations were dry.

When we got in the car, Eddie said, "I've got this big surprise for you!"

"What is it?" Dina asked.

"If I told you, it wouldn't be a surprise!" he answered, a broad smile stretching across his face. "You'll have to wait until tomorrow."

That night we went to his house and had a really nice meal, including some very valuable beans and rice. In the morning, when he came to the hotel to pick me up, I noticed he was dressed better than usual. I was dressed in a Maranatha T-shirt and a pair of cut-off Levis. He looked me over a bit disapprovingly.

"Eddie, should I go back and change clothes?"

"No, we're in a hurry, and you're OK."

We got into his car and drove downtown to the city council chambers, and I really began feeling out of place. Eddie ushered me into a room where there was a very long table with thirty men sitting around it, all of them dressed in suits and red ties. They all rose and welcomed me as if I were David Livingstone, and they had me sit in the mayor's chair at the end of the table—a tall wooden chair painted gold with a bright-red velvet cushion that raised me about four inches above all the others. I felt like a very underdressed king!

When we were all seated again, the real mayor began the conversation. "We understand that you build schools," he said. "We would like you to build a school here in Victoria Falls."

I interrupted him to explain that I was just a volunteer working with a non-profit organization that does build schools, but I was just a volunteer and didn't decide where the schools are to be built.

No one heard or understood a word I said.

"We have two pieces of ground," the mayor said, "that we would love to show you. They are in a planned urban development that we began working on more than ten years ago. We have installed the asphalt, water, electricity, and sewer, but we don't have the money to build a school. One site has five acres, and the other has ten acres. We would like to show them to you so you can choose which one you would like for the new school."

Once again, I went through my "I'm just a volunteer" speech, and I told them that all I could do was to take the information and pass it along. But they were deaf to all my words.

This quickly became one of those special moments in which you keep on keeping on—while praying like Nehemiah, asking God to take over whatever was going to happen.

They drove us out to the first site, and it began to rain just as we arrived. Unless you have stood in a Zimbabwe downpour, you've never seen it really rain. You know how the water pours down in a car wash? That's nothing in comparison to the rain we experienced that day!

The first site was too small for the school, so they drove me to the second site—ten acres of flat, wonderful ground. By the time we got there, the rain had moved on, so the mayor broke out the blueprints they had already prepared for the school campus and showed me where each of the buildings was to go. Then he gave the papers to me, thanked me for coming, thanked Eddie for introducing me to them, and left.

No demands or promises, except that the land was ours to build a school on.

When we got to Maputo, I gave the plans to Pastor Dick, Maranatha's story-teller, and he gave them to the Maranatha leadership team. And in the bustle of stuff that needed to be done, I just forgot about it all.

CHAPTER 21

Eddie and the Safari Thieves

"One day your life will flash before your eyes. Make sure it's worth watching."

—Gerard Way

The day after Eddie roped me into providing a school for Victoria Falls, he picked us up at the hotel and announced that we would be going on a safari in one of his safari vehicles "by yourselves."

We were the only tourists in Zimbabwe at that time. Everyone else was too afraid to go to Zimbabwe, so there was no safari business. No business. None at all! We were the only *mzungus* in town.

A fifteen-passenger safari vehicle pulled up to the hotel, Eddie introduced us to the driver, and away we went—Dina, Terry, and Henry. We safaried for three or four hours in the parks around Victoria Falls, but didn't see many animals. That didn't surprise us, because the people were so hungry that they were killing the park animals for food.

Just as the sun was setting, when we were about fifteen miles from civilization, we suddenly felt like we had dropped onto a movie set. Twelve young men stepped out of the bush, each carrying an automatic weapon larger than himself, each with tattered clothes, empty eyes, and no shoes. They stopped the vehicle and demanded that the driver give them the keys.

The driver refused, and then there was a long heated argument in a language we didn't understand. All this time Dina and I were wondering about our future, confessing our sins, and praying for God's intervention. I remember thinking, *This would be a good time for an angel army!*

"You can't take this vehicle," Henry said. "It belongs to the man back there who has paid for it to go out on safari. You have to talk to him."

All twelve men pointed their guns at us and marched, on the outside of the truck, to where we were seated on the inside.

"Get out of the truck," they commanded.

I was terrified and foolishly tried to defuse the situation with humor and friendship. I held up my camera and asked if I could take a picture of them first. Not a good idea.

In unison, they all grabbed the bolts of their guns, put shells in the chambers, and aimed at our heads.

A really bad idea!

"Get out of the truck," they commanded again.

I put the camera on the truck floor and forgot I had ever owned it. But then I started thinking, *If we get out of the truck, we'll probably be killed or be eaten by the famished lion we heard down the way. If we stay in the truck, they'll probably shoot us. It's about a horse apiece.*

"Why don't you get in the truck, and we'll give you a ride," I heard myself say.

"No. Get out of the truck."

"We're not getting out of the truck," I answered. "If you want a ride, get in the truck, and we'll give you a ride to wherever you want to go. But first, you have to unload your guns."

I don't suggest you ought to try this at home, but it was what God inspired me to say and do as we were talking to the bandits and praying to Him.

The ambushers looked at me like I was nuts!

"Unload your guns and get into the truck."

Not one of them unloaded his gun, but they went off a ways and talked loudly in Shona, a tongue I didn't understand. Then they came back, brandishing their weapons.

"Get out of the truck."

"No. We're not getting out of the truck."

This went on seven or eight times, until they finally started getting into the truck, a couple at a time. Some got in with the driver, and the rest came back and sat with Dina and me.

The guy who sat beside me stunk worse than a Nebraska feed lot. In his lap was half a coffee can with about a dozen fish in it. Each was about the size of a silver dollar and about as thick. There couldn't have been a meal there, even if you had eaten bones and eyes and everything.

We drove silently the fifteen miles back to Victoria Falls, except for our driver! For the entire trip he tongue-lashed the two guys who had chosen to sit up front with him. He was getting after them with a vengeance. I was listening and thinking, *Please, pal, don't get us shot with your arguments!*

When we got near town, the driver stopped and all the guys got out and slunk off into the bush.

"What was that all about?" I asked Henry.

"These men are game rangers and park police," he said, "and they're hungry. Today they killed a zebra, and they wanted the truck so they could haul the meat to town and sell it. I was telling them that if they kill the animals in the park and the economy recovers so that tourists come again, they won't have jobs because there won't be any animals left for them to guard!

"The rangers were telling me," Henry continued, "that they haven't been paid for nine months, and that they are desperate to feed their families. They were hired a year ago at three dollars per month, to protect the animals. But they haven't been paid for nine months!"

The only thing that can legally be taken out of any Zimbabwe park is fish. That's why the one man had the small catch in his lap. Not enough to feed even his smallest child.

We were fully charged as we entered the hotel that evening, but as I look back, I can still feel the angels hovering above the safari truck, keeping the rangers at bay while I requested them to unload their weapons. Those guys were desperate, hungry, and had nothing to lose by shooting the animals *and* us. But they didn't. Angels must have kept them just a little uncertain and finally encouraged them to accept the ride and leave us alone. Even Henry was amazed we were alive!

Over the years, Dina and I have learned that we can't go anywhere without asking God to lead us. We pray for guidance in the morning, in the evening, and a hundred times in between. Often, as on that day, He allows us to get into situations that appear desperate. But He's never abandoned us yet. In fact, I think He smiles whenever He knows one of the hard times is coming because He loves helping us get through it!

There's another thing you might like to know about that safari trip. Henry, the fellow who was driving our safari vehicle, is a member of the Seventh-day Adventist church in Victoria Falls. But we didn't know that!

The day he drove us was his day off. He drove us even though he hadn't had a day off in three weeks and this was to have been his day at home with family. But Eddie had told him that he had VIP *mzungus* coming to town, and he needed his very best driver to work. Henry was so upset about having to drive that he rather hoped we wouldn't find anything worth photographing. Then a herd of warthogs ran past, and Henry pointed them out. "Those are really good to eat," he said.

"What do they taste like?" Dina asked.

"I don't know. I don't eat them."

We started comparing notes with "not eating pigs" and soon discovered that we were members of the same church.

That evening we emptied our suitcases of all the clothes and food we had tossed in "just in case." All the clothes fit Henry's wife and kids perfectly, and the food was like from heaven.

We asked why he was wearing glasses with only one earpiece. Henry laughed and told us that the frame had been that way for three years, and he had learned to balance the glasses so they stayed on. The next morning we took him to a glasses shop and outfitted him with a new pair of frames. That cost us ten dollars. At the end of our stay, he said, "You know God sent you to us, don't you?"

Every time I'm in a Zimbabwe park now, I look at the rangers, hoping to see the face of one who accosted us that night. I'd love to have a serious conversation about his experience, and I'd love to help make sure their families are adequately fed. Even more, I'd like to give each of them a copy of *Steps to Christ*.

Maybe I ought to have Eddie give 'em the books.

CHAPTER 22

Never Alone

*"In the end, it's not going to matter how many breaths you took,
but how many moments took your breath away."*

—Shing Xiong

Nine months had passed since my cancer diagnosis, and Dina and I were living in Livingstone, Zambia. We had been there in January to start three school-building projects, and as soon as we got home, Maranatha called and asked if we would move back for a couple of months to complete the projects. We agreed, remembering that years before, we had told God that if Maranatha asked us to go somewhere for them, we would consider it a call directly from Him. That meant we had no other option, so we moved to Livingstone.

Several volunteer groups had worked for short periods on these buildings, but we had about 140 Zambian laborers working for us every day. They were the core of our work crew. During that time we completed four extra-large block churches, two four-hundred-student school campuses, one smaller campus, and scores of the new one-day churches all around Livingstone.

Cash was one of the big challenges of this job. You couldn't pay the Zambian men with payroll checks, as is done in the U.S. They each needed cash. We didn't have a bank account, couldn't use credit cards for the large amounts of cash we needed, and couldn't pay for anything with American Express.

We were working on at least ten separate job sites all of the time, but we couldn't buy material in advance because we had no safe place to store things. Imagine what would happen to the day's extra construction materials at the end of the workday when 140 laborers headed home from ten different job sites. Those extra materials disappeared! They went home and didn't come back. So, every day was one wonderful challenge after another.

On each workday I had to go to the bank and change anywhere from ten thousand to twenty thousand dollars into Zambian *kwacha* with which to pay our suppliers and make payroll. At that time, the exchange rate was 4,865 *kwacha* to one dollar, and Zambia's largest bill piece of money is a fifty thousand *kwacha* bill, which was the equivalent of eleven U.S. dollars. Just counting that every morning was a major job—and we had to get it exact before we could leave the bank!

I was disgustingly predictable. The first thing I did nearly every morning was to go to the bank. Most of the time I was early enough that I had to wait for the bank to open. When the bank door swung open, an armed guard would greet me and usher me directly into the manager's office. I would tell her how much I needed that day, she would step out of her office, and return a few minutes later and set a pyramid of paper money on her table.

I would sit at the table and count the money carefully under the watchful eyes of the guard and the manager. Once we had confirmed the amount, I would put the money into several grocery bags, and the machine-gun-toting guard would escort me to the car, pat me on the arm, and say, "Good luck!" That's the way we did business in Livingstone five days a week for more than ten weeks. Five days each week.

Typically, Livingstone is a pretty safe town, but at the very time we arrived to work on the schools, a gang of thieves moved in from Lusaka. They did their first robbery the day before we arrived, killing two armed guards and robbing a money-exchanging business. Three days after we arrived, the gang rolled several large boulders onto a road. They caught a woman in their roadblock and then killed a man who stopped to help her. They cut holes in the roofs of buildings just to steal liquor and cigarettes. In general, they filled Livingstone with terror.

I'm sure this gang had their eyes on me. I really stood out. I drove the same vehicle every day, went to the same bank every day, and carried millions of *kwacha* in grocery bags! Yes, we did change hotels every couple of weeks, and I tried to be careful. But Livingstone is a small town. If you're looking for someone there, it isn't likely to take you more than ten minutes to find them.

Yet everything went quite well, so I didn't think much about the danger until the very last day we were in town. That day I visited the proprietors of all the places where we had done business: the hardware store, the grocery stores, and a dozen other businesses. I went to be sure my bills were all paid, but also to say Thanks and Goodbye.

I went into the hardware store where I had done business every workday for two-and-a-half months. After I expressed my appreciation to the manager, he looked around a bit and then asked, "Where's your friend?"

I quickly reviewed all of my visits, trying to remember who might have come with me on one of those days. But I couldn't remember ever coming in with someone else.

"Who do you mean?" I asked.

"Oh, the big guy who is always with you."

I was so blown away by what he said that I just looked at him, speechless.

Outside the store, I sat in my vehicle thinking about what I had just heard. In seconds my head was down and I was muttering prayers of thanksgiving through my tears.

I am never alone. Never! Even on the streets of Livingstone, Zambia, I am never alone. There's a man, a VERY BIG MAN, who walks with me.

When I think about the hardware store manager having seen my angel, I reach my hand out, hoping to touch him. How come he's willing for the manager to see him, but most of the time still hides from me? I guess it's OK. One thing I know is that he's a VERY BIG MAN!

CHAPTER 23

Walking With the Lion King

"After the game, the king and the pawn go into the same box."

—Italian Proverb

The king is here to see you."

"Who? Me?"

It was five fifteen in the morning, and a pink glow was beginning to color the eastern horizon. Dina and I were photographing cheetahs at one of my all-time-favorite-places destination, the Mukuni Big 5 Lion Encounter. It was my good friend Ian who greeted me, squinting as he approached through the breaking dawn. "Mr. Terry," he said, "His Royal Highness Chief Mukuni is looking for you. I have no idea why."

Try as I might, I couldn't come up with a good reason either.

His Majesty Munokalya Mupotola IV Siloka III Mukuni XIX is a much loved and respected chief of many villages and has been for many years—forty-two to be exact. He became king when he was fifteen years of age. He is the man that the movie *The Lion King* was named after. He *is* the lion king.

This day was certainly getting off to an interesting start. We had gotten up extra early to say Goodbye to our friend Basil, the owner of these fantastic cats.

Basil is one of the few people who deserves a book of his own. He's an ex-rugby star who played on teams in half a dozen countries and one of the few white farmers left in Zimbabwe. He's also a wonderful man who has a unique ability to communicate with animals—he has pet lions, cheetahs, water buffalo, elephants, and many more. He has a steady hand, a soft voice, and a no-fear attitude even though he was almost crushed by an elephant.

His unique relationship with animals got started when someone brought him four lion cubs that didn't have a mama. Basil bottle-fed the cubs, let them live in his house with him, and eventually earned their complete trust. I had to laugh when he told me that the most expensive part of raising the cubs was the furniture and drapes they destroyed. When he relegated them to the yard, the meter man stopped reading the meters. A place with four lion cubs patrolling the grounds didn't really need to have the meter read!

Mukuni Big 5 is our friend Basil's dream come alive for those four lions—plus many more lions, cheetahs, and elephants that have been brought to him. He's breeding them to release back into the wild what once was wild. It is a unique interaction between animal and human.

I snapped back to reality when I heard someone asking, "Are you the man who took the photographs?"

It was the chief himself—the lion king; the one and only. It was true that a month earlier I had dropped off some photos I had taken of their cats. The king must have seen them. He asked whether we would we be willing to return later in the day and walk with his royal entourage.

Are you kidding me?

With trusty Canons in hand, I returned later that day for a three-hour walk with the lion king and his companions. Several of the chief's sons, his handmaid

Basil with the four lions that grew up in his house. They are better behaved than most kids.

The lion king and his entourage, Livingstone, Zambia.

and niece, and a famous singer joined us on our lion walk. Dina and Ronnie came too, along with journalists from three different countries. We walked in an unfenced area comprising about one hundred thousand acres with four adult lions escorting us. If the big cats had wanted to run away, they certainly could have. It was a walk I never wanted to end.

No one had a weapon, so if the lions had wanted to eat us, they could have done that too. What we did have for protection was the trust developed between the big cats and the handlers Ian, Sly, Farai, and Aron Tiger Zulu. Martin, Innocent, Brighton and others at the Big 5 also have a rapport with the animals that is nothing short of amazing. These cats behave better than most kids.

I've had the privilege of walking with these magnificent lions and cheetahs more than a hundred times. I like to call it practicing for heaven.

I've learned a few things while walking with lions:

- Lions' skins are ten times thicker than ours, so what they would consider to be a love bite would draw our blood.
- Lions can smell fear, and their instincts say that smells like supper. To avoid that, you must act like you are a part of the pride.
- Lions need love too. They have an unmistakable bond with those who bottle-fed them. When you see them stand on their hind feet and kiss Basil's and Ian's faces, you recognize that to be an act of genuine gratitude, not a trick learned by an unhappy animal.

The lions have accepted me into their pride, which gives me great pride. Mike, Cliff, and the entire staff have become like family, consistently treating us much better than we have ever deserved. Thanks a million, guys! Now, our relationship with them has become a matter of having very good friends who just happen to have lions and cheetahs—lots of them!

We met a lot of chiefs in Africa. The most interesting encounter I had with an African chief began when one who lived about one hundred kilometers from where I was sent for me via messenger. Ronnie and I took the plunge, driving more than an hour into the bush, to a place where we were told we were the first white men to ever visit their village.

The children there were terrified, hiding behind their mommas and crying out as if we were beating them as we tried to approach them. The closer we got, the louder they cried. Finally, one of the mommas came clean. "We've always told our children that if they didn't behave, some day a white man would come from far away and eat them!" Kind of reminds me of a story I heard as a little boy about missionaries ending up in a pot of stew.

We gave some candy away, which led to some interesting scenes. The kids had never seen hard candy or the wrapper it came in. Initially, they put the still-wrapped candy in their mouths and then spit it out. After all, how good does a candy wrapper taste? Once they learned to take the wrapper off, they loved what was left!

Every time we spoke with the king, we first had to kneel and clap three times and then wait for the chief to clap three times in response. The entire village joined in our conversation, sitting on grass mats in a big semicircle with their shoes off, taking in every word. The prime minister of the village was the translator. The chief could understand us directly just fine, but it was beneath him to address us. He would speak in his language to the prime minister, who would translate what he said into English and two local dialects.

The king had asked us to come to his village because he wanted us to build a school in his district. He said he would give us a piece of ground, one kilometer square, on which to build it. The school is now standing, a result of Maranatha's presence in Zambia.

As Ronnie and I drove out of that village at the end of that day, we looked at each other and started laughing. Forty years ago, we would never have imagined we'd have adventures that were this much fun.

First white man? Bring it on!

CHAPTER 24

Bed Sheets and Bottle Rockets

*"How many times do we miss God's blessings
because they are not packaged as we expected?"*

—Unknown

New Year's Eve 1993. What a celebration that was. The fireworks were unbelievable. Bottle rockets ten feet long—long enough that we had to slide them all the way forward onto the dash of our Suburban in order to close the rear door. Engines on them bigger than a two-liter pop bottle. And throw-down M-80s. Those took either courage or stupidity—maybe a bit of both.

Santo Domingo, Dominican Republic, is a rocking place at New Year's time. We were there to build a church, a family project that spanned Christmas and New Year's Day. Our entire family was there, the folks, Shari and John, Susan, and brothers Bruce and Dave. We were staying in a government-owned teachers' retreat near the ocean, living in block buildings with seatless toilets and a stub of a pipe for a showerhead, the only temperature being cold.

Fireworks are sold on most every street corner in the city, the vendors calmly smoking cigarettes while sitting on a pile of gunpowder. They demo their wares right beside their own stands. Each vendor does his best to outdo the others with their homemade bombs.

The bottle rockets were the biggest we had ever seen. We had to stand on a fifty-five-gallon drum just to light the broomstick-diameter bottle rocket that towered above us. Those rockets would take off with a tremendous roar and blow up in a huge explosion at the top of their flight. They looked like Saturn rockets when they took off, and the spark shower was spectacular.

Later that night, we saw fireworks that made ours look like toys. About a quarter mile away, cannons were shooting big military phosphorus flares suspended on parachutes into the air, six or seven at a time. As they reached their apex, the parachutes would open and these battle flares would light up the entire cityscape and ocean bay. Fifty-caliber machine guns were strafing the sky from at least five positions, the bright green and red streaks of tracer bullets making patterns that intertwined as they laced the night sky and rained lead into the bay.

Dina and I decided to walk to the place where the action was. It didn't look that far.

A brisk ten-minute walk down a forested lane bordered on both sides by hedges brought us to the ocean's edge. A large crowd of people had gathered there to watch the government-sponsored fireworks display. It was past 11:00 P.M., the crowd had been partying all day and was rowdy, so we stood about twenty-five feet behind them, trying to not be too visible.

The display produced by the tracers and phosphorus battle flares captured our undivided attention. As the thunder continued, the crowd disappeared—which we didn't notice until we were the only ones on the beach. That produced an eerie feeling, as if someone was in my space, *really* in my space. I looked behind us, and that is when I became almost panicked. Two men were standing directly behind us, and so close to us that I could have reached out and touched them. They were both at least seven feet tall—that's extremely tall in a country where most people stand about five feet, six inches.

The height of these men was intimidating enough, but their dress was even more so. It was unlike anything we had ever seen before. They weren't wearing shoes and were wrapped in inch-wide strips torn from white bed sheets—strips that covered every inch of their bodies, including their fingers, which were wrapped individually. The small slit left open for their eyes was the only part not covered. In the flood of the full moon, the two men stood out like beacons.

When you're in a desperate situation and you don't know what to do, you have to fake it, and that was my only option. So, although I was almost overcome with fear, I forced myself to act. I tried to move quickly, but it felt like I was moving in slow motion.

Reaching into my pocket, I pretended to pull out a pocketknife and open it, and then, reaching even further down into my gut, I let out a tremendous yell and turned to get the jump on the two strangers. There was no way I would win the fight, but trying to do something seemed like a better option than doing nothing.

Adrenaline is a strange animal. It can take you places that courage can't. As I spun around, I tried to make myself look really big and to give out a roar that would wake the dead with the hope of scaring the two men. But when I spun around, they were gone! I had made my move only a few seconds after I had seen the two behind us, but in that time they had vanished without making a sound. We were at least a hundred feet from any vegetation, the full moon was illuminating every pebble on the beach, and there was no place to hide. My heart, running on an overdose of adrenaline, felt like it was about to burst out of my chest cavity.

Dina said she had seen the men too. Maybe they were hiding somewhere between the beach and the place where we were staying. To reach our humble accommodations, we had to make that ten-minute walk back up the forested lane. We were thankful and amazed when we made it back safely that evening. The next day, we asked as many people as we could whether they had ever seen men dressed in strips of white bed sheets. The only conclusion we could reach was that they must have been very bad men. That was the consensus of the street.

Over the years, my mind had repeatedly turned to the strange event on that New Year's Eve in the Dominican Republic, rolling it over and over as I tried to understand what we had seen.

Sixteen years later, I was standing in a warm shower in Temuco, Chile, on a beautiful Saturday morning and that New Year's Eve puzzle came to my mind again. That morning I said a prayer while in the shower, asking for an explanation of the big white mummies. And all of a sudden, the light came on. Why had the crowd dispersed? They'd been as frightened as we were. The two seven-foot-tall mummies had scared them away.

Suddenly I realized the two mummies were our guardian angels. They hadn't come to hurt us but to protect us. By scaring everyone there away, they'd made our walk back to our residence safe. So, no longer needed, they'd disappeared without a trace, not even any footprints. They'd simply vanished.

As I stood in the shower, the warm water cascaded down my back, but my face was wet too—wet with tears of joy, gratitude, and amazement. I was overwhelmed that God cared enough about me to reveal to us our guardians.

Knowing that we are not alone has certainly given us considerable courage in subsequent travels. Would that realization also give me the strength to get through the horrors of cancer? It certainly wouldn't hurt me. If I was needing some visual confirmation of God's care for me, that experience was certainly just what would carry that message. God always gives us exactly what we need.

I still replay in my mind our encounter on the beach that New Year's Eve. Instead of looking for answers, though, now I'm combing the recesses of my mind trying to recall as many details as I can. I wonder how many times those angels have had my back when I haven't turned around?

CHAPTER 25

White Water, Baboons, and the Zambezi

Never let your fears establish the limits of your life.

Our first visit to Zimbabwe was in the summer of 2005. Our oldest daughter, Sheree, was living in Mozambique, and we decided we had better go there to see how she was surviving Africa. Victoria Falls somehow seemed on the way. When we checked into our hotel, we were exhausted from the journey but ready for the adventure.

We didn't have to wait long.

As the sun was coming up the next morning, I was on the balcony, staring at the horizon. The sunrise was colorful, highly decorated—and not just with nature's colors. Brightly colored women's underwear adorned the largest tree in our courtyard, some of it hanging from the top branches.

The baboons were very proficient. The sign on our balcony door read "Please keep your door locked. The baboons are thieves." Some of the clothes stayed in the tree for as long as we stayed in that hotel, as there were no poles long enough to get them down.

The sky was a pinkish hue, as beautiful as I had imagined it to be, the birds were singing and monkeys playing. Warthogs were running down the road from town like a pack of dogs. They'd raided the village garbage cans.

From our hotel we could hear the thundering roar of the falls, which were more than a mile away. As we arrived at the falls, we entered a micro-rainforest ecosystem, the falls producing a steady mist that supported a canopy of jungle cover and ferns. Even though it was a sunny, ninety-degree day, we needed umbrellas as we continued.

At this time of year, the river is down considerably, and people can walk halfway across the more than one-mile-wide riverbed via the Zambian side. It was the place toward which they were walking that had my attention. There were people

The Victoria Falls Bridge over the Zambezi River as viewed from the Boiling Point.
No one who enters the river here lives to tell about it.

sitting in the river on the very edge of the falls. In fact, some of them were looking over the edge. The rock formation they were sitting on is called the Devil's
Bathtub. It isn't for the faint of heart. It's still on my bucket list.

In the eight years that we have been returning to Victoria Falls, we have seen
change, not all of it for the good. In 2004, the *Zim* (Zimbabwean) dollar and the
U.S. dollar were equal. By 2009, it took one hundred trillion *Zim* dollars to make
one-tenth of a U.S. dollar. Not only was there a complete collapse of the mon-
etary system, there was also mass starvation, as food was in short supply. It took a
wheelbarrowful of money to buy a loaf of bread.

Rafting the Zambezi was quite an experience. Feeling a bit of pressure from
my two daughters to not act as old as I looked, I joined them in signing up for
the adventure.

Contrary to what one might expect, the ride is rougher when the water is
lower. The river had just recently been declared "safe" to raft. The entire stretch
we rafted was a class 5 or higher. We walked around the class 6 rapids because we
were told, "Every time people try it, someone dies."

Taking our positions at the front of the raft, we dug in furiously with our
paddles, attempting to have some control. Coming out of the second rapids, our
raft was thrown at least thirty feet high in the air. That's when I learned the first
lesson of rafting the Zambezi: always hang on to your raft. Tumbling through the
air, I could see that I would hit the water long before the raft did.

Upon hitting the water, my mind shifted to survival and to my two daughters, who were also somewhere in the crocodile-infested water. It was the weirdest
thing: I was wearing a beauty of a life jacket, yet I was ten feet underwater and it
wasn't taking me to the top. I opened my eyes to make sure that I was swimming
in the right direction. "Don't panic," I said to myself. What was that they told
me? "Hold your breath and conserve your energy. Eventually, you will surface."

The life vest wasn't taking me to the surface of the water because the water was
filled with millions of tiny bubbles—so many that my life vest was no longer very
buoyant.

Eventually, of course, I did surface. When I did, the waves were scary high—so
high that I couldn't see whether anyone was near me. As the river sped me down-
stream, I realized that rapid number three was upon us. It also dawned on me that
though I had gone on this trip to protect my daughters, I was going to have my
hands full taking care of myself.

Going through the rapids in the water is a rush. Sheree traveled through more
than three miles of river and four rapids before she was pulled out. I covered a lot
of territory myself. We did make it back into the raft, though, and the next time
it went in the air, we all had a death grip on it. We hit the water upside down, but
we at least knew where our raft was!

After riding thirteen of the twenty-two rapids, we climbed out of the river can-
yon on a makeshift ladder constructed of saplings and baling wire. We climbed

straight up for forty-five minutes on this shaky contraption on which one misstep would have taken down the entire group. The next morning we saw our raft guide on the street, walking on crutches. Apparently, in taking the raft down the remaining rapids, he had collided with some rocks, breaking his leg. The Zambezi is a treacherous river, with many areas that are three hundred feet deep.

Once down the river is enough for this old man.

CHAPTER 26

African Bibles

"Do not follow where the path may lead. Go, instead, where there is no path and leave a trail."

—Ralph Waldo Emerson

I love African Bibles. They are falling apart, the spines having been bent so many times that no glue in the world will hold them now. Yet the pages are still holding together, thanks to the glue of faith.

Almost every page is underlined, sometimes in multiple colors; favorite passages circled in red; promises in blue; and commands in green. Every page is worn, with red soil-marks clearly revealing whether the owner is right- or left-handed.

Africans do not carry their Bibles casually, as many Americans do. They hold them close, wrap them in clean rags, or if they know a leather-craftsman, the Bible is honored by a place in a small leather case that holds the owner's most precious possession.

My grandpa's Bible was like that. He always carried it and his reading spectacles in a worn leather case that had lost all its color.

One year we purchased a large box of Bibles to distribute in Africa. We had given most of them away in Malawi, but we had saved seventeen Bibles to give away during the three days we were going to be in Zimbabwe. Each of the Bibles had cost two dollars.

When we got to Victoria Falls, we settled in our hotel and then went down to the craft market. We had been there many times before, talking with all the proprietors and laughing as we disagreed on prices for things we didn't need. We had been away for almost a year, so we went to see what new carvings might be parading in the grass in front of each carver's stall.

The wood carver at the very first little booth we saw when we got out of the car looked at Dina and me and asked, "Did you remember to bring me a Bible?"

We were amazed that he remembered us, and even more stunned that he was standing here asking about a Bible we had discussed in passing more than eight months ago.

"Yes," we said, "but it's still in our room. We'll bring it tomorrow."

That started a flow of Bible requests. Nearly all of the carvers wanted a Bible—far more than the seventeen we had brought.

One of the men, a fellow who says his grandfather can carve anything you want out of stone, produced a slip of paper and a broken pencil and told us we had to start a list of the seventeen "most Bible-needy" carvers. In moments we had twenty-five names on our seventeen-Bibles list.

Then one man came to Dina, pulled her aside, and said, "Please, please, can you give me just one Bible?"

I usually have one extra Bible and thought I might be able to give it to him—until I remembered that I had already given it away in Malawi! Our Bible resources were completely exhausted. No more were available.

When we gave the Bibles to the seventeen men on our list, I told each of them the very same thing: "I will give you this Bible only if you promise to read it."

We got seventeen very serious promises!

Dina said we ought to take a picture of the seventeen men with their Bibles. We took them out behind the shops and took a group picture of them holding their Bibles. They're all smiling and cheering and shouting. It was really cool.

Dina with some of the Thieves Market woodcarvers to whom we gave Bibles.

You know, we have really come to love those guys. Every time we get near a "thieves' market," we drop in, haggle over prices, and buy too much stuff that is too heavy and too large to fit into our luggage. Sure, they're all doing their best to take advantage of us, to get us to pay exorbitant prices for half-carved wattle pigs, but we love them anyway. Maybe laughing together is one of the best gifts we can give them. At least they remember us, even though sometimes I think they remember us as the blonde and the sucker. But when I look at the pictures we've taken in the markets, I realize they remember us as friends—as the people who bring Bibles to them.

And shoes.

The shoe story comes from early in 2012, when Sheree spent a little time with us while we were building a new school campus up by the Botswana road in Livingstone. Sheree is working on a PhD at Johns Hopkins, for which she was doing research in South Africa on AIDS mothers. She had managed to escape work to spend a few days with us in Victoria Falls.

Sheree hates to go to the markets. She says it tears too much out of her heart. But on the last day she was there, she joined a small group of volunteers and bounced off in a minivan to see the carvers. She walked with Brenda for a while, and then with Dina, and then was overwhelmed by a swarm of carver paparazzi who had never seen a beautiful blond woman up close before.

Sheree's a big girl and well able to care for herself, but this group was a little overbearing. One giant carver—who said, "My grandfather is the finest carver in the country, and he taught me!"—did his thieving best to sell her an "ironwood" giraffe that felt like it was actually made of balsa wood. The price started at Lexus level, quickly fell to Chevy level, then to VW, then to Lada, and then all the way down to broken bicycle level. Finally, with a very forlorn frown, he said, "I will trade my grandfather's finest giraffe for your shoes."

Sheree looked down at her bright-pink flip-flops and said, "I need my shoes. I can't give them to you."

The argument went on for several minutes, and finally Sheree said, "I'll give you my shoes, but no giraffe."

Ten minutes later, as we were piling back into the minivan, the carver held his giraffe up to the window. "For your shoes!" he cried.

Sheree slipped out of her flip-flops, and as they drove away, she watched while a big African carver tried to fit into a pair of bright-pink flip-flops.

I hate the begging, but I love the men! They're trying to do their best to provide food for their families.

Whenever you're walking around in a town in Zimbabwe, a little boy will come up to you and try to sell you *Zim* dollars. There was a time long ago when one Zimbabwe dollar would buy a loaf of bread. Then it took four dollars for a loaf. Then ten dollars. Then forty dollars, one hundred dollars, one hundred thousand *Zim* dollars for a loaf, and finally, before the currency collapsed, the government was printing one-hundred-trillion-dollar notes, and you couldn't buy a slice of bread with a whole wheelbarrowful of them. I believe that those hundred-trillion-dollar notes are the largest ever issued by any country—in terms of the number on them. Worthless in actual value.

Last year one young boy came to me with a fresh, unopened pack of one-hundred-trillion-dollar notes. Stupid me, I bargained and bargained and finally bought seventy of them for three U.S. dollars each. I should have bought the whole pack. I don't know what I would have done with them, but this year they're selling for twenty or twenty-five U.S. dollars each! And these were consecutively numbered!

CHAPTER 27

The Crocodile

"Small deeds done are better than great deeds planned."

—Peter Marshall

*N*gwenya is an Ndebele word that means crocodile. In Livingstone, Zambia, it's the name of a village where the poorest of the poor barely exist.

From daybreak till dark, the air around Ngwenya is filled with a cacophony of dull thuds, the sounds of crude hammers breaking granite boulders into billions of gravel-size pieces. The women of Ngwenya tow their children to work with them, teaching them to sit quietly while Mama breaks a giant pile of fist-size stones into a wheelbarrow full of gravel—all in the hopes that someone will come along and buy their pile of broken rock. There are more than four hundred rock crushers at this quarry, all vying for the same customers. If today is their lucky day, they will make a sale that might net them about one U.S. dollar for their day's work; however, most days are not their lucky day.

Karen, our group leader, had visited Livingstone several months earlier. In our subsequent conversations, she had been fascinated by the primitive tools the people were using as hammers to crush the stone: chunks of truck axle, bolts welded together, and misshapen pieces of metal that might have been real hammers long, long ago.

One of the new churches we were building was to be right next door to the rock quarry, and many members of that congregation worked as rock crushers. Karen wondered if we might want to ask the volunteers to bring some new hammers along in their luggage. I agreed and we began sending e-mails to our volunteer work crew.

The new church building that seats six hundred people is by far the finest structure in Ngwenya. I think the entire community came for the dedication service, packing every bench, filling the floor space, and ringing the building with singing supporters. After the service, we asked for all the members who were quarry workers to come forward. You would have loved the looks on their faces as we presented each one with a brand-new, bright-yellow hammer. Ninety very grateful Ngwenya workers went out in dancing from the church that Sabbath afternoon.

The following day I visited the quarry once again—and saw very few of the new hammers. I was amazed, so I asked many of the church members what had happened to the new hammers we had given them. Here's what I heard: "Mister Terry, this is the very first new hammer I have ever owned. I know it will work well, but for a few days I just want to enjoy it looking so beautiful."

Six months later, I was back at Ngwenya. That time I saw a lot of American hammers, most of them looking pretty well used.

When we were working on Ngwenya Hill Church, we had to walk through the village many times each day. There was a family right near the church who lived in a dirt house, with a dirt yard, a dirt fence, and several very clean children. We stopped often to talk about the weather, crops, and food, and to play with the children. We probably were a very bad influence because of all the candy we gave them.

On the night we were leaving, Dina and I stopped to say Goodbye to the family. The setting sun was painting all the dirt a bright rose color. The family was sitting together around their cooking fire, and there were lots of hungry people.

On an impulse, I went over and lifted the lid on the kettle and looked inside, asking, "What's for supper?"

The mother came and looked in the pot with me. There was nothing in it except boiling water.

"What goes in the boiling pot?" I asked.

"Nothing. Tonight we have water, but nothing to add to it."

"Why don't you go get something?"

"We have no money."

"Why don't you have any money?"

"There is no work this week."

"What will you eat tomorrow?"

"We don't know."

We said Goodbye, got into our vehicle, drove down to a corner store, and filled the backseat with bags of mealie-meal and tomatoes, onions, and a few other vegetables. Fifteen minutes later, we were back with our friends, helping to fill the supper pot with more than just boiling water.

A couple of years later, we were back at the Hill Church and stopped to greet our friends. While we were there, Mark Pace, one of our Maranatha volunteers, noticed that the family's chicken coop was empty.

"What has happened to your chickens?" he asked.

"They have all died."

"If we brought you more chickens, could you feed them?"

"We would love to have more chickens," they said, "and we would be glad to care for them."

Mark gave me a "let's go get chickens" look, and before the day was over, we had delivered eighteen healthy chickens to our friends on the hill.

We knew that this family didn't belong to our church, but that didn't matter. As Christians, we have an obligation to help others out, giving back just a little of what we have been given. These folks have become our special friends for life.

You do what you can to try to lessen the guilt you feel for not helping them more.

One of the rock crushers of Ngwenya, Livingstone, Zambia, with the "tool" she uses to turn rocks (behind her) into gravel (in front).

Hard work is no stranger to these people.

CHAPTER 28

Marumba Market

"Courage is fear that has said its prayers."

—Dorothy Bernard

I love the way *Marumba* rolls off the tongue. That was about the only thing to like about the market that went by that name—one of the rougher markets on the eastern edge of Livingstone.

What was it that took us there?

Almost a week earlier, I was driving between job sites in Livingstone, and I came upon a husband and wife carrying three large drums. One was on her head, and two more were strapped to an old bicycle he was pushing. It was certainly a picture. I asked, and they agreed to a photo.

They were heading to the Marumba market to sell the drums he had spent the past six weeks making. At fifty thousand *kwacha* a piece (US$10), they were a bargain.

That night I shared the photo with Dina and Ron. I think it was Ron who said, "Terry, you need those for your house." He was right! It was the weekend, and we flew from Zambia to South Africa to spend two days with our oldest daughter, who was living in Johannesburg. I kind of forgot about the drums for almost a week, and then Ronnie reminded me of them.

I started asking around about the Marumba market, but no one wanted to give us directions. One evening, after a long day of work, Ron, Dina, and I drove down a twisty road we had never driven before. Livingstone was much bigger than we thought! It was almost dark by the time we parked our vehicle alongside the road—practically the only vehicle we could see in a market that covered more than six square blocks.

I had all my camera gear and all of our cash inside my backpack. I couldn't decide whether it was safe in the truck, so I put it on my back and the three of us started walking, asking as we walked along whether anyone had seen a man selling three large drums. The answer was always the same, and we kept on walking, through stands that held fish, produce, dry goods, and almost everything else that a person could imagine.

Except for drums. This was not a tourist market, and there were no drums for sale.

We certainly were the only white people there. And what a sight we were! Me, an old guy with a big backpack; Dina, a blonde with another backpack full of cameras; and Ronnie, a.k.a. Tarzan.

Why would we call a great guy like Ron "Tarzan"? Because that's who I think of when I look at him—from his shoulder-length hair to his deep tan and rugged build, he has the rock star look. Our friendship goes back to seventh grade, and we've never had an argument. Ron might look scary, but he has a heart of pure gold. I'll never forget the time he gave his helper his shoes because the helper needed them more. Ron continued to work barefoot till we found him some shoes. Yes, he is a rock star in my book, and one fun guy to be with.

As we walked through the Marumba market and asked about the drums, the people there started asking us questions as well. "White man, what are you doing here?"

Looking them straight in the eyes, we responded, "The same thing that you're doing here."

When we'd been asked this question about six times, Dina looked at Ron and me and said, "Let's get out of here." It was after 11:00 P.M.

The next day I asked one of our workers about the Marumba market. "It is a very dangerous place even in the daytime," was his reply. "I wouldn't recommend that you go there. It isn't a good place for white people."

Right after supper that evening, Tarzan and I headed back to the Marumba market. Dina had had enough and stayed at the hotel with our valuables. This time we had printed a picture of the man and wife with the drums. The locals couldn't believe their eyes. What were these two crazy *mzungus* doing back here?

By the time we got out of our vehicle, there was a crowd of more than seventy people. They asked why we had come back. We showed them the picture, and it was passed around. Everyone shook their heads, except for one guy, who said, "I know where the drums are. Follow me." Without another word, he began to walk away from the market.

We walked down several narrow alleys and through some really dumpy areas, and just when Ron and I were looking at each other and thinking, *This is bad,* it started looking really good, because right in front of us were two of the three drums I had seen more than a week earlier.

Where was the guy who owned them?

He had rented the place where they were stored for fifty *kwacha* per day (about 1.2 U.S. cents) from the woman we were now talking to. But she hadn't seen him all day. She owned a cell phone, so we gave her twenty thousand *kwacha*, about

The drum maker and his wife.

four U.S. dollars, and asked her to call us when the owner of the drums arrived. She agreed. Another ten thousand *kwacha* went to the man who had taken us to the drums. He was delighted to have made a day's wage in thirty minutes.

At about twelve thirty that night, my cell phone rang and a voice said, "He's here." I went down to Tarzan's door, and within five minutes we were heading to the market.

We had to park by the road and walk quite a distance. We wondered what all these people were doing up. There wasn't much light at that time of night, just an occasional bare bulb outside a shack. No one in this area had the money to light the night.

As we got closer to the place where the drums were, we could see the woman standing outside to greet us. "Here he is," she offered, pointing to a small pile of rags beside the drums. "He was so drunk when he got here that he just passed out," and with that she began to massage his side vigorously with her foot.

It took a few minutes for the old drum maker to respond. When he finally woke and saw me, he was delighted and started singing and dancing around us, giving us kisses on the cheek. It was one of those moments that even MasterCard can't buy.

As we walked back to our vehicle, each of us with a three-foot drum resting on a shoulder, we marveled at the thought that we would be on such an adventure in Africa and building schools and churches together—friends for more than forty-four years. It was 2:00 A.M.

* * * * *

The story should have ended with the last paragraph above, but sometimes there are lessons to be learned. One is that we should never want anything too badly. I woke up at 5:00 A.M. the next morning. After all, we had places to be and schools to build.

But what was that horrible smell? Had I stepped in a big cow pie and brought it in on my shoes?

No. Instead, we had carried it in on the drums. The drum maker had used it quite liberally to draw the rawhide tight. So, the two drums stood guard *outside* our hotel door, and they had more than six baths before we could bring them into our home.

We must have had some adventurous angels with us that night. Maybe they will even want to have a word with me about it some day. That would be welcome!

CHAPTER 29

"Where Are My Sweets?"

"Most of the shadows of this life are caused by standing in one's own sunshine."

—Ralph Waldo Emerson

Livingstone, Zambia, has become my favorite Maranatha building destination. I can well remember our first trip to Livingstone in 2005. We walked the seven kilometers from Victoria Falls to Livingstone. It was one of those sweltering hot African days without even a breath of wind. The only road to town from the old Victoria Falls Bridge was unpaved and was covered with dirt so fine that it swallowed our shoes as we trudged along.

There wasn't much to Livingstone at that time. A few small "restaurants" that were best described as a few tables in someone's backyard. We found a taxi to take us back to the bridge that spanned the gorge. At the time I certainly wouldn't have thought that Livingstone, Zambia, would eventually become our second home.

In January 2010, Maranatha began a huge building effort in the Livingstone area. When Karen called from the Maranatha office asking if we would like to go to Livingstone, we were thrilled. Not only were we getting to travel with Karen once again, we were going back to Africa!

For those who have traveled with Karen, she needs no introduction. Her planning is meticulous, often including amazing hotels and excursions; fantastic chefs and inspiring spiritual leaders. Karen can maneuver through a minefield and look good doing it. We always consider ourselves blessed to be on projects with her and sometimes her family.

When we got to Livingstone, we found that what had been a sleepy little village five years before had grown in leaps and bounds. A new airport is well under way; the road from the falls through town and on to Lusaka is now paved; and new shops and hotels were springing up everywhere. The need for schools and churches had grown along with the town.

We arrived with a large crew of volunteers—more than 160—and we had close to a hundred locals working for us as well. Our assignment was at least as big; we were to build a couple of primary school complexes, four large churches, and many bush churches—eventually, close to one hundred buildings total.

Fortunately, I had some people who gave me really good help supervising all these projects: Brother Bruce, Nick, longtime friend Ronnie "Tarzan" Priest, Big John, and Kent, just to name a few. "Delegate or stagnate" has long been a motto I believed in, and this was a good time to put it to the test. With more than 250 people to keep busy at numerous job sites, keeping supplied with the materials that they needed was a challenge.

I had an old Toyota pickup that proved useful for circulating around town, going from job site to job site. There were a lot of roadblocks in town, where the police checked for licenses, registration, insurance, and whatever else they felt like. I was getting stopped a dozen times a day, sometimes twice in one short drive. In the course of the first three weeks, I kept my papers on the dash of the truck; they were more necessary than fuel was.

When we returned home from that project, Zambia was still in our hearts. We were wishing that we could have stayed longer. We didn't know that our wish was about to come true.

Less than two weeks later, we were again occupants of a pressurized metal tube, on our way back to Livingstone. This time we were to stay just shy of three months. Tarzan Ronnie had also returned, and Livingstone was beginning to feel like home.

Our first stop after checking into our hotel was at the supermarket, where we bought several small bags of candy for the kids. We hadn't driven six blocks when we hit the first police roadblock and heard again the familiar "License and registration please."

This time, though, instead of reaching for my wallet, I reached into the bag of candy and handed several to the officer. A big smile crossed his face, and with a wave of his hand, he said, "You can go." That was so easy. We knew we needed to try this approach again and again and again. In the following two and a half months, we were stopped hundreds of times, but not once did we have to produce any paperwork. We were the candy suppliers to the cops.

Late one afternoon, the friend I called Tarzan and I were bumping along a dirt path of a road out in the middle of nowhere, giving one of our workers a ride home. When we rounded a bend, we came upon a police checkpoint. No one had told us that this was bootleggers' alley.

Ron and I struggled to fasten our seat belts, but the road was so rough that we couldn't pull out enough of the retracted belts to fasten them. We pulled up to the checkpoint red-faced, still trying to buckle up.

"Where are my sweets?" demanded the officer. I was so shaken up that it took a while for his question to sink in. Since I didn't respond, he spoke again: "Traveling without seat belts is an offense that calls for a three-hundred-dollar fine for each of you. Pay now, or go to jail."

The police have pistols, but prefer to sport a bit more force. Intimidation is a big factor here.

Ron and I looked at each other and began to reach for our wallets. Neither of us had three hundred dollars with us, but we had to go through the motions. As we sat there holding our wallets and returning the officer's gaze, there was a really awkward moment of silence. We were both surprised by what happened next.

In a very kind voice and with a slight smile on his face, the officer said, "You can go, but next time I want my sweets!" Feeling tremendous relief, Ronnie and I burst into laughter. So did the officer.

The very next day we were on the opposite end of town and came upon the same officer at a different checkpoint. "Where are my sweets?" was the first thing out of his mouth. I handed him a big handful, but he looked inside the truck anyway. "I want the whole bag," he announced.

"Sorry," I replied. "If we give you all our candy now, we won't have anything to give you the next time we see you."

"You're right," replied the policeman. "Come back soon!"

Dina and I have made many trips back to the Livingstone area. We always stock up on hard candy when we go. It's been more effective than a driver's license, and who doesn't need new friends?

CHAPTER 30

Kenneth

*"What lies behind us and what lies before us are tiny matters
compared to what lies within us."*

—Ralph Waldo Emerson

*I*t's something I'll never forget. Our Maranatha volunteers, along with a small group of local workers, were busily building a new school complex in Manja, Malawi. He was watching. Under one arm he carried a small cloth satchel, glistening with years of human sweat and body oils, its corners so worn that just a few threads kept things from falling out the bottom. The zipper had broken long ago, so the top of the satchel was tied closed with tightly knotted rags.

I assumed that he was one of the job seekers who often came by late in the day. But as I looked at him, something about his gaunt figure called out to me. I needed to know his story.

However, we were busy and it was late in the day, so I turned back to my work. The next time I looked up, he was gone. I felt a pang of guilt, but what could I do now?

That pang was reinforced when I joined the volunteers on the bus and rode back to the hotel. Dina's voice broke deep into my thoughts: "Did you see that man—the one by the road?" she asked. She didn't have to describe him any further; I knew exactly whom she was referring to and was glad she also had noticed him.

For the next few hours, we were busy with supper, worship, and planning for tomorrow. Lying in bed that night, Dina and I talked again about the lonely figure we had seen beside the road. We had lost an opportunity to make a connection, and we prayed that God would give us another chance.

The following day was the Sabbath. Right beside the school we were building was a five-hundred-member Seventh-day Adventist church. This Sabbath it looked like all the members were in attendance and had brought their neighbors.

Terry and Kenneth basking in the glow of a new friendship.

The church was packed, and several hundred people of all ages were sitting on the floor, while others were sticking their heads in through the windows. The late-latecomers stood farther back outside, straining to catch every word.

As usual, my Canon camera was in my hand, and I was searching the crowd for the perfect picture. From my vantage point near one of the front doors, I noticed how the light was intermittently shining on the face of a darling little girl sitting on the floor at her mother's feet. Her mother was singing in the choir, and the girl was where Mom could keep an eye on her. Occasionally, the small coloring book in her hands became a reflector, bathing her face in warm light as if she were in a portrait studio with the best lighting money can buy. Getting a picture without her reacting to the camera was tough, but she finally grew bored with me and went back to coloring. That's when I got the best photo!

From there I went to the other side of the church and took pictures of Pastor Dick telling a story about how God plans for our needs far in advance. The kids were mesmerized by the story, but the local interpreter provided the greatest fun. It was almost as if he were competing to see if he could tell the story with even more gusto and vigor than Pastor Dick was using. I've heard Pastor Dick tell a lot of stories, and I'd have to say that this day he met his match. Listening to those two storytellers, no one wanted the story to end, not even me, and I already knew the story!

As the seventy-five kids found their way back into the congregation after the story, I slipped outside of the building, hoping to find a little bit of a cool breeze. I walked around the corner, toward the entrance, and then my heart skipped a beat—maybe two.

There, sitting on the steps of the church with his back to the doors, was the same thin man Dina and I had noticed yesterday. He sat tightly pressed against a newly painted wall, picking at a small patch of paint on the side of the church. It was obvious that he was hoping no one would notice him, or worse yet, ask him to leave. Beside him lay all his earthly possessions—three items: the small satchel that I had noticed earlier, a cornmeal bag, and a stick with rags tied tightly around it.

I wondered how long it had been since anyone had recognized him as a human being. My mind flashed back to Bible times, when the lepers were to be ignored and avoided at all costs.

But Jesus loved those lepers!

The Holy Spirit gave me an uncontrollable desire to sit down beside this man, put my arm around his shoulder, and give him a genuine Nebraska hug.

When my hand touched his shoulder, I had to resist the urge to recoil. Placing my hand on his shoulder was like putting it on a surface that was sticky with honey, but that smelled like a Nebraska feed lot. Kenneth—that was his name—was wearing four T-shirts, each one stained with sweat, grease, dirt, and who knows what else. When I eventually removed my hand, it, too, was sticky and smelly, but by then I didn't care. I had made a new friend—one of God's favorite people.

Kenneth's feet were a size eight, but his shabby tennis shoes were a size eleven. He'd stuffed them with plastic bags to keep them from falling off his feet as he walked. More rags were tied to the gaping holes in the shoes and wrapped around his ankles. Socks were useless, as the bottoms of his shoes also had holes. He was a pitiful figure of humanity, yet his eyes showed a flicker of life.

We talked for quite a while, and I was glad that he spoke good English. Kenneth was fifty-eight years old, my age. In fact, our birthdays were less than a month apart. I loved seeing his face light up, and having him feel free to place his hand on my knee, which is the African way of showing full acceptance.

I asked Kenneth why he didn't have a home. He told me his story in a soft, halting voice. He had lived on the streets of Blantyre, Malawi, for more than two years, never having a bed or a shower; choosing a different gutter each night to keep the thugs from robbing him of what little he had left. A soup kitchen in town had kept him alive, but there were thousands of others like him there also waiting for that same piece of dry bread. When Kenneth was lucky, he would get a small meal of corn mush or stale bread. That happened only once every two or three days.

"Life wasn't always like this," he said, his head bowed in sadness and shame. "Three years ago, I was a very successful businessman in Harare, Zimbabwe. I owned a dream house with my own car out front. I was earning more than all but the top ten percent of people in my country. It was not easy. During the day I worked as a scribe in the magistrate's office. In the evening I hoed the weeds and carried water for our garden. My wife ran a produce stand downtown where all the locals shopped, and she always sold out by the end of the day."

Zimbabweans are industrious people. With much hard work, Kenneth and his family were living a good life.

"Then the elections came. No one really wanted to vote because we already knew what the outcome would be. The opposition party had won two previous elections, but each time the ruling party refused to step down. When the new elections came, everyone had to vote. The town keeps good records, and you could be escorted to the polling booth rather roughly if you didn't find your way there by yourself."

As I listened to Kenneth's story, I felt a tear form in my eye, and I pulled him a little closer.

"All my family, including my parents voted, and we all voted the same way: we voted for change. But we didn't get the change we expected. Within weeks both my mother and father were dead. The only crime they were accused of was voting for the wrong guy—the one we knew was really the right guy! Three weeks later, I came home from work one night and found my wife and two children, both in their early twenties, with bullet holes in their heads. That's when I decided that it would be better to be homeless than dead."

Kenneth left home that night, not even taking time to bury the dead. Knowing he was also on the killers' list, he walked toward Malawi.

Malawi was more than five hundred miles away, and Kenneth walked every dusty mile, eager to escape his past. Everyone knew the magistrate's scribe, so he had to walk on the less frequented paths and through miles of dangerous land. Three weeks later, Kenneth "vanished," like so many others, into Malawi.

I sat on the church steps with my arm around Kenneth, overwhelmed with the simple fact that *it was only by the grace of God that I wasn't in Kenneth's shoes.* None of us can control where we are born. All we can do is control where we go from there.

I asked Kenneth if I could pray for him, and he gladly accepted. I could barely get any words out, and I don't think I prayed a very good prayer. With our heads pressed tightly together, we bonded as one and became brothers. Strangely, I think I was much more concerned about Kenneth's situation than he was. I was already thinking about how we could get him a good meal, new shoes, something to deal with his head lice, a shower, and a dozen other "needs" he had.

Kenneth wasn't thinking any of those thoughts. He was just basking in the pleasure of being recognized as a human being and knowing that someone cared.

There was a big church potluck next door at the new school, and with a bit of encouragement, Kenneth agreed to join us. He nervously went through line, doing his best to be invisible in his tattered and smelly clothes, yet the stench overpowered even the strong odors of beans and *shima*.

After lunch, we took all the food we could find that would last a few days and filled some small paper bags "to go." He checked the pockets of his tattered khaki cut-offs and found one that hadn't developed a hole yet. That's where he put the small wad of Malawian *kwacha* that I had handed him. It wasn't much money, but it would help him for the next few days. Kenneth didn't count it for fear that someone might see the money and rob him later; he just nervously glanced around while pushing the *kwacha* deep into the pocket. Others saw what we were doing and joined us, giving him candy, boxed juices, and apples—almost enough to open his own roadside food stand.

As we prepared for bed that night, I was troubled—enough that Dina noticed. She looked at me and said one word: Kenneth. I fought back tears as we talked about the millions of Kenneths who live in this world, and we had done a poor job of helping even one. Some things in life are not fair. Kenneth's situation was just *wrong*.

The next morning as we gathered our bags to leave Blantyre, I found Susan Woods, wife of Maranatha's country director for Malawi. Susan's mango and fresh coconut ice cream would win the blue ribbon in any food show bar none, but what's especially good about her is that she is one of the most compassionate people I know. I asked Susan if she knew Kenneth, and she thought she remembered seeing him near the Manja church. We left money with her to buy him a new pair of shoes, a mat to sleep on, and food. We also emptied my suitcase of shirts and socks and of anything else we had that might fit him.

Two weeks later, we received a treasured e-mail from Susan. One of the local Maranatha workers had tracked Kenneth down and worked it out for Susan to give him the gifts. When he received the bed mat, Kenneth fell on it and praised God for His blessings. "This is the first time God is blessing me like this," he said. "I am so happy."

When Susan showed him new shoes *that fit him,* he couldn't believe his eyes! And then when she gave him the old army duffle bag filled with a blanket, sheets, shirts, more clothing, soap, a toothbrush, toothpaste, and flip-flops, Kenneth said, "This is so much more than food—my heart is no longer hungry."

Susan also gave Kenneth a well-worn English Bible, a gift that instantly became his most prized possession. When the members invited him to become part of the church family, he quickly accepted. "I will no longer have to sit on the steps and wish I was family. Now, I belong."

Our experience making friends with Kenneth reminds me of one of my favorite quotations: "You can't live a perfect day without doing something for someone who will never be able to repay you" (John Wooden).

CHAPTER 31

The Pearl

"The greatest use of life is to spend it for something that will outlast it."

—William James

*W*hen my good friend Garwin McNeilus asked if I had an interest in Uganda, I instantly knew that the answer was Yes. The very name, *Uganda,* brings so much history and so many adventures to mind: Idi Amin, Uganda's murderous dictator of the seventies. The mountain gorillas that live silently in the country's deep forest. The mass of human refugees that were caught in the conflict in neighboring Rwanda, the homeland of the Hutus and the Tutsis. The lush and wild Great Rift Valley that runs through the country. *Uganda.* To many, it is known as "the Pearl of Africa."

Garwin has led hundreds of building projects all over the world, and this was going to be one of his biggest. We were to complete seventy buildings in less than a year, all of them designed to bring new life and respectability to Bugema Adventist University. This university was founded in 1948 as a major training center for Seventh-day Adventist students from all over Africa. The school is living up to its purpose; currently, more than five thousand students are enrolled, representing nearly every country in Africa.

Our seventy buildings would include dormitories, staff housing, classrooms, bathrooms (with flush toilets and showers), a cafeteria, and a modern kitchen. I was privileged to make three trips to help construct these new buildings.

Due to travel schedules, we always arrived in Uganda well after midnight. The late hour made our welcome even more impressive. On each of our visits, the administrator's wife had prepared for us a special, homemade feast. She is an awesome cook, making everything from pizza to guacamole, and her banquets are about the nicest reception meals I have ever had the pleasure of eating.

Before the Maranatha volunteers joined us, we had about forty Ugandans helping us every day. They were excellent workers, and continued to work with us until the last lawn had been seeded. We simply could not have done this job without them.

The university has Internet service, but the signal is difficult to capture. One evening I was sitting on the corner of the administration block trying to catch a hint of Internet, when a muscular young man came by and asked if he could help. Hoping his luck would be better than mine, I welcomed his offer, and we walked around the campus together hoping for an Internet miracle. No such luck! But what I did discover was far more valuable than a few moments on Facebook.

I learned that my new friend, Adam, had been a Muslim most of his life. For several years, his life had been exceptionally good because a local Muslim cleric had provided him with a car, a laptop, clothing, and a hefty allowance to cover his tuition, food, and housing. Adam was the guy who went to the big tree in the center of the campus three times a day to call all of his Muslim brothers together for prayers. He explained that he and several other Muslim students had been planted in the university to encourage the worship of Muhammad.

Adam's story was compelling. I soon forgot about the Internet and sat down to listen as he wove his tale.

Adam said one of the school's Bible teachers had taken a special interest in him, asking him hard questions that had made him think about God, values, and commitment. After many weeks of questions and Bible studies, Adam decided to accept Jesus Christ as his Savior and to be baptized as a Seventh-day Adventist Christian—a momentous change in his life!

When his fellow Muslims learned of his decision, they were so incensed that they came to the university and took away his car and all his belongings and told him that if they ever saw him again, they would kill him for becoming an infidel. That same day his fiancée left him and his parents spat on him and told him that they never wanted to see him again.

Accepting Christ had become a really rough spot in Adam's road. One day everything had been very good, and the next he was a Christian with nothing left to his name. He had lost his family, his fiancée, and all means of financial support. He had gone from having *everything* to having *nothing*.

Adam went to the manager of the university's cafeteria and asked if he could have the scraps of food that were left on the plates, and he offered to wash the dishes in exchange for the privilege. The manager agreed, and Adam worked late every night, washing pots and pans and cleaning the kitchen and dining area. After a month, the manager told him that he had been doing such a good job that the cafeteria was going to give him a small wage in addition to permission to eat the table scraps.

Other challenges kept him on guard. His brothers hated him so much for becoming a Christian that they contracted with a hit man to kill him. The assassin had come to the campus a few weeks earlier and found Adam studying alone in the library. When Adam saw a heavily garbed stranger coming toward him and

Terry and Adam.

noticed the clothing bulging oddly, he realized this person was there to kill him.

Thinking quickly, Adam addressed the stranger and said, "Allahu Akbar"—an Arabic saying that means "God is great." If one Muslim says this to another who is a stranger, and the stranger doesn't immediately return the greeting, he is an enemy. Adam spoke the greeting clearly and waited for the response, but none came. Instead, the stranger continued to walk toward him and began to reach under his robe for his weapon.

Adam sprinted for the door with the stranger hot on his heels. Once out of the library, he ran toward a nearby crowd of students, and soon realized that the stranger was no longer pursuing him. Although God had saved him that time, he wondered what might happen next!

Adam told me that when he had become a Christian, he had gained much hope in his life, but he had also lost much and was becoming very discouraged. When I heard his story, I wondered how I might be able to help. Then I remembered the business card a friend had given me when I was receiving treatments at the Eden Valley Lifestyle Center. Reaching into my wallet, I found the card and gave it to Adam. Jeremiah 29:11 was printed on the card: "For I know the plans I have for you, . . . plans to prosper you . . . and give you hope and a future."

We sat together on the campus that evening, talking about the plans God has for each of us. Then—and I will always remember this—Adam's eyes moistened

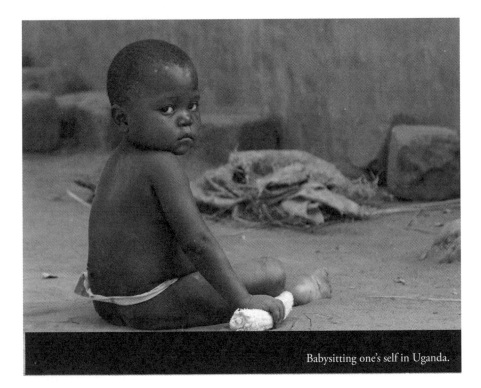

Babysitting one's self in Uganda.

and he put his big brown arms around my neck. "I woke up today with no family," he said. "Now I have one of my brothers back!"

I am honored to be part of Adam's Christian family.

The next time I went to Uganda, Dina came along. She had done some shopping for slacks, shirts, socks, and shoes that we thought might fit Adam. When we went to his room, we discovered that he was wearing the only clothes he owned. As Dina spread out the new wardrobe, she was officially dubbed "Mom," and I was upgraded to "Dad." The next day Adam sported a new wardrobe that made people ask if he had gotten an inheritance. He was proud to tell them, "Yes!" He had inherited a new mom and dad!

Adam is an industrious student. He had secured an additional job on campus—he was now cleaning the bathrooms in the men's dorm. Every time I looked him up, he was either working in the dorm, working in the cafeteria, attending classes, or studying. It seemed as though he never slept.

Adam completed a program in theology at Bugema Adventist University and has begun to share his newfound Christianity with the Muslim world. The risk of his being killed is astronomically high because his opposing his former religion makes him a marked man. However, Adam faces an even bigger risk—the risk of not fulfilling God's plan for his life. With the conviction that God is leading him to be a missionary and a pocket full of faith, Adam has stepped out to make the world a better place.

He's an amazing guy. One day he's helping a widow find food for her family, the next he's hauling water for someone who is ill, and the next you may find him scrounging scraps of food for a friend who is hungry. He is determined to give his best to meet the needs of others, often putting their needs before his own. He is a wonderful model of Christianity, helping those who cannot help themselves.

Ochieng Bernard Ouma is another of the extremely pleasant students we met at Bugema. Ochieng's skills as a leader became obvious as I started assembling work crews to construct the new buildings. One team had a crew of five muscular men, including Ochieng. I began to teach them the mechanics of forward and reverse on a screw gun. The screws, screw guns, and steel were all completely new to the five fellows. This wasn't a common method of construction in Uganda, nor was the concept of precision measuring and fastening.

I was surprised when I found that half of our local helpers had studied the Pythagorean theorem, but not one of them had ever seen a screw gun. More than once they spun the screw the wrong way, but by the end of the day they were all looking pretty smart. It was fun to work side-by-side and watch fear and prejudice be replaced with trust and friendship. Any of the guys in my team could become construction leaders. I really hated telling those guys goodbye at the end of that trip, even though I knew we would be back again. I went through my suitcase and gave away almost all of my clothes. In return, they humbled me once again by presenting us with a going-away present of loofah sponges.

Thanks to the marvel of Facebook, I've been able to stay connected with many of my Ugandan friends. It's rewarding to think that I might have been the spark that encouraged them to achieve their full potential. Ochieng and some of his friends have formed their own nongovernmental agency to help widows and orphans in their country. Their vision, and their determination to get things done, puts me to shame! To be truthful, I don't think any of us really reaches the true outer boundaries of our potential. Most of us are too afraid to fail and never really become all that we could be.

Our last trip to Bugema was the most memorable. Our group included a number of friends who had built one-day structures before. Some of our group—Bruce, Pete, and Charlie—own construction companies or construction-related businesses. God really impressed the right people to come on this project.

We arrived at Bugema on a Wednesday, but the three containers filled with our building materials were still held up somewhere in customs. That meant we had to regroup and come up with an alternate plan of construction.

The alternate included fencing, landscaping, pouring sidewalks, and constructing septic systems. We worked feverishly on these for the next two days, and then cheered Friday afternoon when three large trucks arrived carrying our twenty-foot-long shipping containers. A giant boom truck offloaded our precious cargo that afternoon and that was about all we had time to do before sundown.

We dedicated Sabbath to going deep into the bush to visit a village no white person had visited for the past three generations. The photo opportunities were wonderful! The first portrait I took was of an old man, who after having his picture taken, proclaimed, "I must be someone of great importance for you to come all this way to take my picture!"

Yes, my friend, you *are* someone of great importance. As one of God's kids, you are valued more than riches.

My best picture that day came when I asked to be introduced to the oldest woman in the village. Everyone knew who she was, but no one wanted to disturb her. "She sleeps a lot and is very grouchy when she is woken up," they said. "If we disturb her, she will be even worse!"

Eventually, though six of the young men agreed to take me to her hut. They said I would be on my own, once they got me there.

When we reached the far end of the village, the six young men pointed to a mud hut ten feet in diameter, and then they disappeared, not wanting to be caught in the crossfire. The door was slightly ajar, so I gave it a light knock, and about thirty seconds later the door swung slowly open.

The interpreter who was with me for the day ducked under the thatch overhang and went into the nearly pitch-black room. I followed, but couldn't see a thing. Then the door swung ever so slightly open, allowing a sliver of light to come into the room and illuminating the woman's face as perfectly as if I had staged a portrait session in an expensive studio.

There was no bed. The woman was lying flat on the floor—no pillow or sheets, just the polished clay floor. As my eyes struggled to adapt to the dark, my mind raced to figure out how I could get a picture of the woman in this dark room without using a flash. I would have to use a very slow shutter speed, and so I crouched down and braced myself so as to make myself the best human tripod possible.

It wasn't quite that easy. Grandma was unhappy about being awakened. She was even unhappier because she was hungry and had a headache. My picture would have to wait. First, I had to establish a relationship.

I apologized for waking her up in the middle of her afternoon nap, and I gave her some of the chips and hard candy that were in my camera bag and some money so she could buy medicine and food. But the most important thing I did for her was just to listen. It seems that no one else wanted to listen to her anymore! The longer I stayed, the nicer she became. She finally gave me permission to squeeze off a few frames of her face as it was bathed in a beam of soft afternoon light. It was quite wonderful.

As we walked out of her hut, she asked if we would be coming back the next day and every day thereafter. My translator said she was wondering aloud if we might be angels sent to help her. That certainly made me think. I know that I'm just a guy, but she wasn't so sure.

Saturday evening we opened the containers we had been so anxiously awaiting. Clint, who had helped load the steel into the containers before they left the factory in Minnesota, took a big bolt cutter and cut the locks. Everything was there, and we began unloading, stacking, and sorting our steel.

At about eleven o'clock that night, I tripped and fell, breaking my right wrist and dislocating my right shoulder. Dina and Renee wrapped my wrist and shoulder with duct tape and cardboard and drove me to the "local" hospital, which was in Kampala, about an hour away.

Kampala is the capital and largest city in Uganda, with a population of about two million. Idi Amin, Uganda's president, had his own hospital built there, the best in the country. That is where we went—only to discover that their only X-ray machine was broken, or "blacked out," as they phrased it. A trip to a tiny clinic across town finally netted us a marginal X-ray, but no doctor was there to read the results or set the bones. We returned home as the sun was rising. It was a really short and painful night.

God truly had sent the perfect team on this project. We had loads of talent but no egos. And there was no milling around wondering what to do; this team went straight to work. As Garwin would later jokingly put it, "The broken arm helped get Terry out of the way so the others could get something done."

By the end of the week, this amazing team had assembled two containers of materials. That's nearly eighty-thousand pounds of steel! From those materials they had built sixteen buildings, some of which were sixty feet long.

There are often new volunteers on each trip, and it is interesting to see how

The oldest woman in the village. She said no one listened to her anymore.

God calls people to His service. Quinn and Jessica are a perfect example. These two really neat Christian young adults had decided to plan their honeymoon around a mission trip and were praying about where to go. I happened to drop by their shop in Lincoln while they were still deciding. They shared their dreams with me, and I realized that our Uganda trip could be an answer to their prayer. The connection we made almost seems too perfect to have happened by chance.

"Come with us to Africa" just kind of fell out of my mouth. Without missing a beat, they looked at each other and said, "We're in." As a bonus, they brought Michelle, Jessica's sister.

We had a really great time working together in Uganda. My favorite picture of the entire trip is of Jessica giving her pink sandals to a very poor little Ugandan girl. While helping the little girl put on her new sandals, their heads touched, and I could feel the love flowing from ten feet away. It was a powerful moment for all of us.

Our group took more than four hundred pounds of clothes to give away, and we were in awe seeing how the recipients acted like each piece was manna from

Jessica, on her honeymoon, makes another love connection.

heaven for the recipients. People like Michelle, Jessica, and Quinn are the future of missions. It is refreshing to see young adults get their priorities right. Yes, there is a place for us old folks too—that's one of the beauties of a Maranatha mission project. All ages come together as family on the project.

Renee is another volunteer whose life was up-ended on the trip. We have known Renee for more than twenty-five years, and when she said, "I'm going with you," we were pleasantly surprised. Renee was so determined to be a part of this trip that she sold her pickup truck to finance the travel costs.

There are more than five thousand students at Bugema, but Renee was really taken with the two young men who were helping her build retaining walls around the school's sidewalks. They talked as they worked, and Renee discovered that bicycles would make their lives much easier and better. Obviously, the fellows couldn't afford new bicycles—in fact there were no good bicycles on the campus! So Renee asked around and found a way to go to Kampala, purchase the bicycles, and bring them to Ronnie and Peter.

I think it was Renee who was being blessed as Ronnie and Peter raised their new wheels to heaven and exclaimed, "Thank You, Jesus!" Doing something for someone who can never repay you is a powerful thing.

Renee has signed up with Maranatha to go back to Africa again. She says she's going even if she has to sell her vehicle again to afford it.

My broken wrist? Two days later, I finally saw a doctor who knew what to do with the break and sprain. We had gone back into town on Sunday, only to discover that the clinic had lost our X-ray, and they said they couldn't take another one. So, back again on Monday. This time we saw a specialist who took a new X-ray and put a nice plaster cast on my arm. Since two days had gone by, it took two very large people to help him set the wrist. One pulled on my hand and the other pulled on my elbow! That really got my attention. In fact, it made me sweat a bit. OK, it made me sweat a lot!

The bill? A whopping fifty-six U.S. dollars. Finally I was free of my lovely cardboard splint.

Prayer was certainly a part of this trip. I'd been feeling a bit discouraged a few days before Garwin called. Yep, it can happen to any of us. I was thinking that the last foray in Zimbabwe had been bit of a challenge. Maybe I wasn't up to international service anymore. So, it was time for another fleece.

My cancer indicators had been tripling every month. Not a good sign. So we prayed that if God wanted us to continue our international travel, my monthly cancer count test would show a drop. And I had just received a lab report showing a slight reduction in PSA—exactly the fleece I had asked for—the morning Garwin called.

And having my phone ring an hour after I got that lab report and to be invited to go to Uganda certainly didn't feel like an accident. It felt more like God was saying, "Go back to Africa."

We also quite literally prayed ourselves out of Uganda. On the last day of our adventure, we all visited the source of the Nile—a series of huge springs out of which flow millions of gallons of water per hour.

At certain times of the day, the drive through Kampala can be rough. The intersection ahead of us was a convoluted mess of five roads all coming together. We couldn't see it, but we knew it was there. However, a solid mass of taillights stretched as far ahead of us as we could see. Our two-lane road was carrying five lanes of traffic, three of them going our way. Except we weren't moving. Not even a little bit. We were hopelessly stuck in a sea of taillights. And we had a flight to catch.

After thirty minutes of not moving even an inch, Ronnie, a.k.a. Tarzan, stood up in the bus and announced that we were going to pray. I loved how he went around to everyone asking that their hearts be in our prayer. He said it worked better that way.

Tarzan's prayer went something like this: "God, this is where we need You to take over and take charge. Please help us get to the airport."

With that, the bus started moving. It was as if God had parted the Red Sea of taillights in Uganda. We drove several blocks—until we were approaching the problem intersection. Then, once again, we sat and waited, while precious minutes were ticking away.

After about twenty minutes, Ronnie could take it no longer. Standing up again in the bus, he announced that we were once again going to pray. He announced it so loudly that three guys on a motorcycle jammed in next to us leaned into our bus. They asked, "Could we pray for you? What do you need?"

Then one of the guys on the motorbike offered a really nice prayer. And then Tarzan's voice could be heard once again: "God, we need to get to the airport," and with that our bus started moving again. This time it didn't stop for any great lengths of time; we kept steadily moving forward.

Coincidence?

Maybe. But I don't think so. I think Ronnie's faith was rewarded as a result of his humbling himself to ask for help. The faith of the rest of us was also strengthened.

Even with a plaster cast on my arm, I was able to keep clicking my camera. I did miss many pictures, but the few I got were special. There were so many good people pictures, of both volunteers and locals. I would have had to stay another month to get everyone's picture.

One photo does stand out. It is of our campus guard. He is wearing a hooded, fur-lined parka, is balancing an oversize LED flashlight on his right shoulder, and is cradling in his arms a giant wooden bow and wicked-looking arrows.

We were safe in Uganda!

Our night guard while living in Uganda.

CHAPTER 32

"I Have PayPal"

"Success is to be measured not so much by the position that one has reached in life as by the obstacles which one has overcome while trying to succeed."

—Booker T. Washington

Peru is the land of the Incas, and it is home to at least eighty-three of the 103 micro-ecosystems found around the world. Of course, that means that Peru is one of the most diverse and amazing countries in the entire world, and it is certainly one of our favorite destinations. Dina and I have been fortunate to explore the deserts, jungles, and mountains of Peru, from Lake Titicaca to Lima to Pucallpa.

Lima is the driest city in the world—ten times drier than Cairo, Egypt. The locals will tell you that it *never* rains in Lima. We were in Lima when it rained for the first time in twenty-eight years. It amounted to a tenth of an inch. The best hotel in town leaked like a sieve! Why would you spend money on waterproofing when it never rains in Lima? My cab driver summed it up by saying, "In my twenty-four years I have never seen rain fall from the sky." All this seems so strange for a city sitting right on the ocean.

Pucallpa approaches the other extreme. It's one of the wettest places on earth. Set in the midst of the headwaters of the Amazon River, it's a city of green jungles and brown rivers.

Way back in 1965, our good friend Clyde Peters carved an airstrip on one of the banks of Pucallpa's Ucayali River. This home airstrip was in an extremely primitive area, where rivers were the only roads, and they were usable for only part of the year.

Clyde reached out to the indigenous peoples by making medical relief flights into areas that were so remote that they could only be reached by air. As you can imagine, some of the tiny airstrips the local people cleared for Clyde's plane gave even the experienced jungle pilot cause for extra prayers. In 1975, the Peters family moved back to Nebraska.

Others continued to fly planes from the home airstrip until 1989, when the Maoist Shining Path guerillas began to operate in the area. The home airstrip was abandoned to weeds and snakes, but natives in the distant villages continued to maintain their tiny strips for eight long years, hoping that one day the metal bird in the sky would return.

In 1997, word came that the political climate had changed and that it was again safe to step foot onto the airbase. Clyde and his son Alan immediately put together a group to rebuild the base. Clyde asked us to join him, and that started us out on one of our favorite mission adventures.

Two of the base's staunchest supporters, Molly and Beto, were there to greet us when we arrived in our little wooden boats. Beto is a pilot and mechanic—a rare but wonderful combination for flying in the jungle. Molly runs the radios, cares for the base, and takes care of the hundred and one other things that come up every day. On that first trip, Molly also served as our cook, taking way better care of us than we deserved.

Jenni asking us to buy some of the Shipibo tapestries she has woven.

Our plan was to replace some roofs, replace screens on the windows, and splash paint on some buildings that had not had human inhabitants for a very long time. It was unbelievably hot, but great fun. Sloths hung from the trees around the airbase, the local children were eager to show us their pet parrots and ocelots, and we had fun counting the number of dinner-plate-size tarantulas we evicted from the decaying buildings, though we eventually lost count.

Early the first morning, a crowd of natives came to our camp and spread out their flea market of wares: clothing, artwork, bones, teeth, beads, pelts, and seeds. However, you couldn't buy any of it! The artisans and collectors wouldn't have been interested even if I had held up a one hundred dollar bill. Theirs is not a money-based society. So we put away our money and went back for our suitcases. The women who had the goods were adept traders!

I came back with my suitcase, found something among their wares that I wanted, and then let them pick through my suitcase until they found a fair trade. I traded away almost all my clothes on that first trip, returning with the clothes on my back, and with their clothes and artwork in my suitcase. When we arrived at the Lima airport, I surveyed one of the gift shops. There, on a very special rack, was a dress similar to one I had in my suitcase. The price tag was US$990!

"Why is this so expensive?" I asked.

"The price is very high," one of the clerks told me, "because Shipibo artwork is some of the most primitive collectable artwork in the world."

Go figure.

So began what became multiple journeys to Peru. Though we've traveled to many different areas in there, it's Pucallpa that we keep returning to. We've been there on mission trips during which the volunteers have built a school, improved the airbase, and even built a small medical clinic. It is such a neat location, yet it has so many desperate needs.

Over the years, we have watched money gradually infiltrate its way into the jungle economy. First, it was one dollar bills. They had to be perfect. If they had a mark on them, or if they were torn, the traders didn't want them. But if they were perfect, the traders would bargain for them zealously. When I asked the indigenous people what they were using their money for, assuming they were using it for food or clothing, they said, "No, that would be completely wasting it. We use the money to send our children to school in town so they can find a better life. When they find a better life, they tell us about it, but they never return here to live."

Modern culture is decimating their society, yet they know it is for the better. As a result, they have a love-hate relationship with money and the strangers from far away who bring it. Improvement is truly a two-edged sword.

The last time we were leaving Pucallpa, a very slender twenty-eight-year-old woman said, "Mister Terry, please buy something from me. I really need the money."

Jenni was one of the first people we had met on our first visit fourteen years earlier. She was the sweet little girl who had followed us to the airport, wearing the clothes we had given her. Every time we went back to Pucallpa, we looked forward

Shipibo traders have traveled for miles hoping to make a sale.

to seeing Jenni. She was such a treat.

Now she was a mother of four, with big responsibilities, and she was asking us to buy something from her because she needed the money. She wasn't asking for a handout. She wanted to do business.

I looked at her and said, "Jenni, I am so sorry. I am completely out of money."

Without batting an eye, she said, "That's OK. I have PayPal."

I could hardly believe my ears. PayPal in the jungle? "How do you know about PayPal, Jenni?" I asked.

"If I take a wooden canoe and go three hours up-river, I can get to PayPal."

Unbelievable to me! "OK, Jenni," I said. "We are going to buy something from you."

That day we bought two hundred dollars' worth of things we didn't need to help four kids who needed our support. When we tried to pay her, she discovered that she was only set up to pay, not receive! A friend of ours was going back to Pucallpa a few weeks later. He found Jenni and settled our debt.

Even though we have seen tremendous change in just a few short years, there is still a desperate need for emergency medical and support flights from Pucallpa to scores of small villages in the headwaters of the Amazon. These flights are still being carried out by the good folks at peruprojects.org.

With Jenni, her sister, and the kids.

CHAPTER 33

Welcome to the Jungle

*"Until you make peace with who you are,
you'll never be content with what you have."*

—Doris Mortman

Before we leave the headwaters of the Amazon, we really need to take a wooden dugout canoe ride up to the tiny fishing village of San Francisco. It's a couple hours boat ride if the water is high enough—the Ucayali River is the highway.

The river is busy this time of year; it's as full as it gets. There are as many boats on the river as there would be cars on a highway, the river being more than a half-mile wide in many places. It finally narrows down into smaller tributaries and huge expanses of water covered with a small green algae that we cut a path through, only to have it fill in behind us as if we were never even there. The long-shafted Briggs and Stratton pecky-peck, four-stroke, homemade boat motor announces its presence as it cuts a path with its homemade propeller.

Kids are playing in the river as their mothers wash clothes in its muddy water. How they get their whites so white is beyond me. Once you leave your boat, it's a steep climb up a muddy, slippery bank, but steps have been carved into the slope starting about halfway up. At this point, I'm wondering which is the lesser evil, muddy shoes or muddy feet.

The village greets us with long drying racks built of reeds and loaded with hundreds of sun-dried piranha. This village has no telephone or power lines, and no road connects it with other villages or the rest of the country. The river is the only highway.

The kids run around naked, and the adults still wear the Shipibo dress—bright colors and unique designs, most all on handmade cloth, dyed with colors found in nature. No two designs are ever the same—something about fooling the spirits.

At the top of the hill and the far end of the village is an Adventist church built by Maranatha volunteers. It's not real fancy because all of the materials had to be transported by canoe: the metal roofing, the truss materials, everything. The side walls are native grasses woven into mats.

The worship service there rivaled that of the finest church I have attended. These people know how to worship. The offering plate is filled with dried fish and produce, with a few *pesos* thrown in. Each week the head elder takes the produce three hours down the river to town, where he sells the goods. The proceeds then are turned in to the local conference.

The next morning we were in for a treat as the village elders agreed to take us on a fishing expedition. It was four thirty in the morning and still as dark as ink when they paddled up to our base. Our boat was a hollowed log about forty feet long; really, a long dugout.

We didn't go far from our camp. When we reached the fishing site, one of the men slipped into the water without making a sound, clothes and all, right up to his chin—he kept his ball cap dry. This man was holding a fistful of the fishing net. As we made a big circle, feeding out more net, it became apparent that the man in the water wanted to get back into the canoe sooner than later. As he climbed into the canoe, the other three men pulled the bottom of the net closed and then they began to pull it into the canoe.

As the net began to accumulate in the bottom of our canoe, the fish began to stack up. Lots of them. Hundreds of piranhas—enough to eat a herd of cows. Six different kinds of fish that looked like big prehistoric catfish, with long tentacles that would paralyze you for up to two days if you touched them. The scariest of

A wooden dugout boat ride through the swamps and rivers of the jungle.

all was the *machachu,* a fish one meter (about three feet) long that had wicked-looking teeth more than two inches long. When it bites, it locks its jaws and won't let go till the flesh tears.

The men were now shouting in Spanish, "Step on their heads before they bite your feet off!" By the time the last of the net was hauled in, we were standing ankle-deep in fish, the friendliest of the lot the piranha. The men were working feverishly to grab the fish with the poisonous feelers and break them off on the gunnels of the boat. All of the fish had teeth; the only difference was how big. We were certainly stepping quickly; tennis shoes didn't offer much protection.

Glad to be back on shore, we went to the kitchen for breakfast. The fishermen made a big fire outside; I really didn't think much about it, they were probably cold from being out at that time of day. The sun was just now finding its way onto the horizon.

Breakfast really hit the spot. We'd been up for three hours and had worked up a pretty good appetite doing the two-step out in the canoe. As we were finishing up the meal, the screen door swung open and one of the men picked up four plates and set them down in a row on the table. Then another man solemnly placed the machachu on the plates. "You killed it; you must eat it," they declared.

That fish was big enough to feed eight people. I ate what I could and shared the rest with all who were brave enough to eat it. The water where it had been caught wasn't exactly pristine, to be sure. But the whole experience had been an adventure, and it was all seared into my mind forever, culminating with the machachu that still seemed to be threatening me, wicked teeth and all.

My youngest daughter, Terra, provided one of the highlights of my Pucallpa adventures. It was while we were there that she committed her life to Christ, and Pastor Eddie baptized her in the Ucayali River right by our camp. He did the honors as the piranhas circled.

Here are a few things we learned about living in the jungle:

+ If you see orange balls of fire coming toward you at night, run in a zigzag—it's harder for the crocodiles to follow.
+ If you swim in the Ucayali River, wear a T-shirt to prevent the piranhas from nibbling off the small appendages on your chest.
+ If killing a rat in your condo is in order, make sure you have a big enough broom.
+ Never put your hand in the water when you're on a boat, you might catch a fish.
+ Jaws lives here.
+ A cold shower is a lovely shower.
+ There are a thousand eyes in the jungle; you are never alone.

CHAPTER 34

The Sacred Valley

"Happiness is something that comes into our lives through doors we don't remember leaving open."

—Rose Wilder Lane

One of my favorite Peruvian destinations is the beautiful Vilcanota Valley, called by the locals *"El Valle Sagrado,"* the Sacred Valley of the Incas. The valley enjoys a pleasant, sheltered climate, and it's in a fertile area that the Incas took full advantage of, scattering towns and agricultural centers throughout its length. The star attractions of the valleys are the lofty Inca citadels of Pisac and Ollantaytambo—massive fortresses that proudly preside from elevated positions on the side of the mountains.

This beautiful valley is also the route of the narrow gauge train that runs to Machu Picchu, which has been the only way you could get to Machu Picchu other than by antique Soviet helicopters. Machu Picchu deserves a chapter all its own—this fantastic granite fortress built atop a cliff, the stones with which it was built so precisely cut that a credit card won't fit in the joints between them. Machu Picchu poses two mysteries: First, how were the stones cut so precisely? And second, how did the builders get the stones from the quarry, which is almost two miles away, across the raging Urubamba River and then straight up a mountainside?

We had come to this part of Peru to build a church in Urubamba, a church that had interesting roots.

A very old lady lived in the Sacred Valley. One night she dreamed that an Adventist church was to be built in her town of Urubamba. It was to be built on a piece of ground that she owned, right beside the ancient Inca trail. It's one of the most visible sites in the town. And since most of the town is hundreds of years old, having a vacant lot on the main street was indeed a very big deal.

The following morning the old woman told her daughter, Maria, about the dream. Maria agreed to forward her mother's request for a church and offer of a lot to Maranatha.

The church was built of concrete block and was to have a metal roof. Our part of the construction, laying the concrete block, took five days. Then part of our team traveled to Pisac to paint another recently built Maranatha church.

The weekend turned out to be a highlight for all of us. Most all of the volunteers had brought new kids' shoes and socks to be given away. Karen had arranged for us to have a Communion service on Friday night, the twist being that we would wash the feet of the village kids and outfit them with new shoes.

As we looked at the feet of the kids before us, a lot of thoughts went through our heads. Did we really want to touch those dirty feet, which had walked countless miles on the dirt trails around us and were battered and scarred and crusted with dirt? Most of these kids had never had their toenails trimmed. That was a task in itself.

As we immersed our hands in water made dirty by those little feet, it became obvious to us that this is what Jesus would have done. It was a joy to warm the hearts of those children and to let them know that they are loved. And every child without exception walked away with new shoes tucked securely under their arms, more than four hundred of them. They were going to keep those shoes looking new, if just for a little while.

Here's a story about a funny thing that happened on the trip. The second morning we were there, three of us met for breakfast, compared notes, and decided that our maids had commandeered our belts for their own use or maybe to sell. That was disturbing, and we let the front desk know.

The following morning all was well—our belts were hanging neatly from the closet poles, announcing their return. Dina didn't fare quite as well, though. She had a small bottle of hairspray that she used in the morning. But this particular morning, she found, strangely enough, that the more she sprayed, the limper her hair became. The hairspray in her bottle had been replaced with water. After she attained a sewer-rat look, we glanced at each other and broke out laughing. It was all we could do. We still laugh about it.

By the way, how many people can you fit into a VW minivan? We can attest to the fact that the answer is at least twenty-nine. That's how the taxis roll in the Sacred Valley.

Machu Picchu—an amazing stone village built on a mountaintop surrounded by cliffs.

CHAPTER 35

Who Stopped the Rain?

"The only way of finding the limits of the possible
is by going beyond them into the impossible."

—Arthur C. Clarke

One of our favorite Maranatha trips each year is the one we take with the Kansas-Nebraska young adults. One year, we went with that group to Santo Domingo de los Colorados, in the heart of the Ecuadorian jungle.

The road from Quito to Santo Domingo is a winding, dangerous mountain path. The road is carved out of sheer stone cliffs on the sides of green mountains that reach above the clouds. Rockslides and landslides are common, especially when it rains. This road is widely acknowledged to be the most dangerous road in Ecuador. It is also the main corridor to the coast, so it is heavily traveled by trucks and buses piled high with chickens, pigs, and goats.

A light rain began to fall as we left the Quito airport. Quito is at an elevation of 9,350 feet above sea level. As we descended into the rainforest, the rain fell harder, the drops becoming bigger and beating a steady cadence on the windshield of our bus. Then fog set in, and the air, which had been giving off the fresh fragrance of jungle rain, started to smell like overheated brakes, *our* overheated brakes!

Ecuador has two kinds of bus drivers: city drivers and mountain drivers. On this trip, we had a city driver on a mountain route. As the curves became sharper and the descent steeper, the brakes smelled hotter and hotter. Did I mention that this road doesn't even have a shoulder? It's just a narrow ribbon of used-up asphalt clinging to the side of the mountain.

About two hours into our mountain adventure, a tremendous explosion rocked the front of our bus. Our right front tire had blown out. As our bus driver fought to keep the bus under control and bring it to a stop, he looked like a rodeo rider trying to hold on to a raging bull. We crunched to a halt at one of the few places on a hairpin curve where there was actually room to pull off and change the tire. In fact, it was one of the only places on the entire road that was big enough to pull anything over, much less a bus.

I jumped out to help get the wheel changed and was amazed at what had caused the tire to explode. Our city driver had gotten the brakes so hot that the center of the steel wheel was glowing orange, and the valve stem had melted.

We very carefully removed the red-hot wheel and the remains of the tire from the bus and rolled it out into the rain, where it continued to sizzle and pop. Twenty minutes later, it was still too hot for any of us to touch. I got to wondering that if this had happened to one wheel, the other front wheel might be in a similar shape. We collected water bottles and poured all the water we could onto the wheel and valve stem of the other front tire.

As we were waiting for the wheel and axle to cool down, a car going the opposite direction from us pulled up. The driver rolled down his window and shouted through the rain, "How did you know about the terrible rockslide three kilometers ahead?"

I listened to the conversation and realized that God had just performed an "avoidance miracle" for us. If the tire hadn't blown, and if we had been careening on down the road, we could have arrived at that corner just as the rockslide reached it. The rockslide could have tossed our busload of volunteers over the cliff, and we would have become another set of statistics about the most dangerous road in Ecuador. Instead, we were alive and eager—thirty-eight of God's kids off to build a church. I still wonder if God put a city driver in a mountain bus to help us avoid the rockslide.

Whatever the case, we sat on the edge of the road for several hours, until a bulldozer arrived, cleared the rockslide, and opened the road so we could continue to Santo Domingo, the fourth largest city in Ecuador and home to more than three hundred thousand people.

The next morning we arose to a heavy sky and the fragrance of soon-to-arrive rain. As we piled onto the bus, the heavens cut loose with a torrential downpour that pounded like drummers on the roof of our transport. The rain was driving so hard that no one wanted to get off the bus. Walking through that rainstorm would have been like walking through a car wash!

The bus driver spoke quietly, his broken English grabbing our full attention. "When it rains like this in the jungle, it usually rains for five or six days. You won't be able to work today." Pronouncement finished, he emphatically switched off the ignition key, and one by one we made our dash for the hotel door, only forty bone-soaking feet away.

The hotel manager wasn't any more encouraging. "When it rains like this in the jungle, it rains for a week or more. I have lived here all my life. I know the weather, and this is the rainy season." With that he walked to the front entrance of his hotel as if to confirm his weather forecast and to watch as his parking lot became a swimming pool.

We were all pressed into the lobby, and the kids wanted to change into dry clothes as soon as possible. But then a little voice inside my head said, *"Pray."* It simply seemed like the thing to do.

Elder Jim Hoehn said a short prayer that went something like this: "God, we are here to build a church for You. If You want that to happen, we are going to need Your help and some dry weather."

When Jim said, "Amen," I heard myself say, "Let's be on the bus in five minutes." The kids looked at me as if I had lost my mind, and then most of them slogged back to the bus without changing their clothes. We got as wet getting on the bus as we had getting off. Then we told the driver to start the engine. "We're going to work," we said. It was an audacious step of faith, but that's what people on these trips learn to do.

As we pulled out of the parking lot, the rain was hitting the windshield so hard that the wipers couldn't keep up with it. The worksite was about a fifteen-minute drive away, and the closer we got, the more the rain let up. As we pulled into the gates of our worksite, the rain quit and the sun came out.

Early morning prayer circle at the church we built in Santo Domingo.

The change in weather was good, but our job site had become a lake. We distributed shovels and in a few minutes had made ditches to drain off some of the water. By the end of the first day, we had laid four courses of block all the way around the building. We were back on schedule.

Clouds covered the sun and rain began to fall at five o'clock, as we boarded our bus for the hotel. It rained hard all night and was still raining when we stepped out in faith by getting onto our bus in the morning. Once again, we drove through heavy rain almost all the way to the job site. As we entered the job site, the rain stopped and the sun came out. Then that evening, as we boarded our bus for the hotel, the rain started again. The weather continued to follow this strange pattern every day—except the last day.

For us, the last day was no different than all of the others. We drove to the job site in the rain, and the rain stopped as soon as we arrived for work. Our work went smoothly, and we finished the building completely. We even installed the metal roofing and got all of our scaffold and planking cleaned and stacked. As we boarded the bus that evening and began the drive back to our hotel, we were *immediately* in a heavy rain.

The hotel manager was waiting for us in the lobby. "Where have you been all day?" he asked.

"We completed the church project," we replied. "We'll be worshiping there with our church family tomorrow."

The expression on his face spoke even louder than his words. "I've been driving around town most of the day, and it has been raining really hard all day everywhere I've gone. Santo Domingo has gotten more than four inches of rain today, but where you worked, it was dry?"

We must have been in a bubble all week and especially that Friday. God's bubble. He knew how badly we wanted to finish what we had set out to do. With His help, we had reached the goal.

Sabbath morning we woke up to the singing of birds and a big orange ball glowing on the horizon. It was a perfect day for the dedication of our new church. With much fanfare, singing, and speeches, the keys were handed to the pastor, and another Maranatha church was complete.

What a powerful statement was made that week as we stepped out in faith every day, driving to work in the rain. How many of us fail to claim the promise of grace just because we don't want to drive through the rain to get it.

CHAPTER 36

Blowguns and Trophy Heads

"The tragedy of life is not that it ends so soon, but that we wait so long to begin it."

—W. M. Lewis

One of the most enjoyable aspects of going on Maranatha mission adventures is what we call excursions. These times of exploring jungles, photographing wild animals, and wandering through ancient ruins add a unique dimension to Maranatha trips. This Sabbath afternoon was no exception. Forty-five minutes from town there is an ethnic group called Tsachila, "the men with the red hair." Every man in the community shaves the sides of his head and styles the remaining hair into a helmet-like shape, which he then turns red with grease and the seeds from the achiote plant.

The story behind this tradition is fascinating. Hundreds of years, ago a smallpox epidemic struck their tribe. When the situation became desperate, the shaman directed them to beat achiote seeds into a mash and cover their bodies with it as though it were a healing salve. The bizarre prescription warded off the smallpox, and for many years it was the tribe's custom to paint their bodies red—in fact, so red that when the Spaniards arrived they thought they had discovered a new race of humans! Their hairstyle today, bright red and shaped like the achiote bean, is a tribute to the medicine that saved their tribe.

The Tsachila are not your normal Ecuadoran tribe. Until very recently, they have been headhunters, and they're still eager to show you their collections of the shrunken heads of their enemies. Less than ten years ago, a missionary came to their village, gave the chief a Bible, and told them about Jesus. They liked what they heard, gave up head-hunting, and adopted the love of Jesus.

Even though they no longer hunted heads, they were very happy to show us the process they had used to shrink heads. First, they removed the contents of the head, and then they sewed the skin tightly back together. The finished result was a head about the size of a tennis ball, but the head retained all the features of its former owner. It's a great size for hanging from a person's belt—or the mirror of a car, if they only had one.

We had a great time as the men taught us how to throw their spears and shoot their blowguns. They set up big targets, and we threw spears at them until our arms ached. Then they brought the eight-foot-long blowguns out. At first I thought trying out these weapons would be only a guy thing, but even the girls enjoyed blowing feathery darts.

As the sun began to set, we were pleasantly surprised when the village leaders asked us to join with them in a large circle. Then the chief brought out something wrapped in cloth. Then, with much reverence, he unwrapped a very well-worn Bible, their only tangible connection to God.

As the chief read a few verses and we sang a few songs, it was evident that we were all in this together. Even though we live on different continents, we worship the same God. The world had become a bit smaller to us, and we had made some interesting friends.

A former headhunter blows a conch shell to mark the end of the day.

CHAPTER 37

Green Mambas

"Life shrinks or expands in proportion to one's courage."

—Anais Nin

*D*ina hates snakes. She really, really hates snakes.

When we first started talking about maybe, possibly, on an outside chance of going to Africa, Dina always demurred. "I don't want to meet a snake in Africa," she said.

We had been asked to help build a school near Beira, Mozambique, and I think Dina finally agreed to go just because Sheree was working in South Africa and we would be able to see her. All the way, in the car, in the plane, in the airport, and in the car again, she prayed that there would be *no snakes*!

After completing the building project, we took the volunteers on a safari to Mozambique's Gorongosa National Park, a vast wilderness at the southern tip of the Great Rift Valley. Though once seen as "Africa's last Eden," the Mozambique civil wars have decimated the animal population to the point that the park had become land without animals. "Maybe," I mused, "all the snakes are gone too!"

No such luck.

We stayed in a wonderful little grass-thatched chalet that seemed safe from snakes. But when we went out on safari the next day, our driver began telling green mamba stories. If he had been telling stories about rattlesnakes or even cobras, it would have been better. But all of his snake stories seemed filled with this snake, which is one of the most poisonous snakes on the continent.

"My friend and I were traveling through Gorongosa Park in an open Jeep," our talkative guide spouted, as if he were giving a lecture to second-year biology students. "He was a dangerous driver because he loved killing snakes. Whenever he would see one crossing the road, he'd slow down and see if he could skid the tires right on the snake. He thought it was a great challenge and a great sport."

That was about enough of the story for Dina, but our guide went on, seemingly unable to stop without telling the whole story.

The guide pointed down to the clutch pedal on our safari Jeep and continued. "My friend the bad driver saw a very large bright-green mamba snake trying to get across the brown road up there by the trees. He hit it hard, slammed on the brakes, and then spun the wheels, trying to chew up the green mamba really well. But instead of chewing up the mamba, the wheels threw the snake up through the floor right where the driver would step on the clutch while shifting gears.

"This was a feisty snake," continued the guide, "that didn't want to be chewed up. When he was thrown into the car, he slithered right up the driver's cowboy boots and bit him just above the boots."

"What happened then?" asked Dina.

"He pulled off the road, and in ten minutes he was dead."

Dina was horrified, with all of her worst suspicions confirmed. "You could be bitten by a green mamba, even while driving down a road inside a vehicle!" She was ready to go home now, before supper!

When we got back to camp, it was almost dusk, and the snake story was taking a backseat to hunger. We put our gear in the chalet and got ready to walk down the road to the restaurant. Since the stars were bright, and supper was only about two blocks away, I decided not to take a flashlight.

I opened the outside door of our chalet and stepped down onto the concrete

The mango market on the road to Gorongosa. There were lots of sellers, but not many buyers.

step and then onto the gravel path. As my foot hit the gravel, Dina screamed. It was a scream that would have awakened the dead! Long, high-pitched, and desperate.

I spun around and saw my wife standing on the porch and pointing her flashlight onto the narrow step I had just walked across. What I saw just about stopped my heart! The light of her flashlight was illuminating a three-foot-long green mamba that was stretched out on the cool welcome mat on our porch—right where I had stepped. The snake was in the center of the porch, and I had missed it by no more than an inch. But there had been life in that inch! I couldn't believe my eyes, and even with Dina continuing to scream, I gave my angel a quick nod for making sure my big, clumsy foot missed the snake. Then I tried to decide what to do next. I looked around for a weapon, but all I could find was a very weak six-foot-long stick.

The snake, now very aware that we disliked it, tried to crawl past Dina into the chalet. That did not go over very well, so I took my stick and began "coaxing" the green critter away from the door.

Mr. Mamba became angry and took it out on the stick. He struck my stick thirty or forty times with lightning speed and accuracy, breaking the stick in half. I grabbed both pieces, terribly aware that my protection was now only three feet long.

The snake stood up to face me, and just then Dina slammed the door, leaving me fully in the dark. Not a good thing.

I yelled, "Open the door—I need light!"

When the light came on, the snake was gone.

I checked under the doormat, around the steps, under the chalet—everywhere. Nothing! No green mamba anywhere.

So we went to dinner, hoping they weren't serving anything green.

We told everyone our story, and one of the guides said, "Oh yes. We have green mambas. When you see one, you must catch it and then release it far away from your chalet."

He gave me a snake-catcher—a mechanical arm with grabbing jaws on one end. I slept with it right beside our bed.

The next morning we opened the door slowly and looked around very carefully before heading down the trail to breakfast. As we approached the restaurant, I noticed that there were four locals drinking coffee on the veranda about four feet above the trail. Just as I raised my hand to greet them, a six-foot-long green mamba shot across the trail right in front of me. There was no time to use the snake-catcher.

"Is he green, sir?" one of the men called out to me in Portuguese.

"*Sí,*" I responded, and immediately all four of the men jumped up from the table, leaving the coffee there, and dashed off toward another building.

Thank God, I thought. *They're going to get help.*

Sunset in Gorongosa National Park

When the men had gotten about seventy-five yards away, one of them stopped and called out to me: "You should run, sir. He can run faster than you!"

We sprinted into the restaurant, thanked God for protection, and ordered breakfast.

Later that day we met the cleaning ladies who were to care for our chalet. They were standing outside and refusing to come in. They pointed to a small bush beside the doorway. "A pair of green mambas live there, sir. We can't come in and clean your house because we know they will kill us."

Here's what we learned in Gorongosa about green mambas:

> ✦ They can kill a person with one bite.
> ✦ They can slither along on the ground faster than a person can run.
> ✦ They are so aggressive that if they see you, they will try to kill you.
> ✦ If you ever kill one of a pair, the other will find you and . . .

Other than that, they're just snakes.

We were stuck in that place, so we stayed in that chalet for the next two days with a pair of green mambas eighteen inches from our door. But I believe angels stood between us and the quick green death.

It was crazy, but kind of fun.

CHAPTER 38

Johnny

"Life is a grindstone, and whether it grinds a man down or polishes him up depends on the stuff he's made of."

—Josh Billings

Some things cannot be forgotten. Johnny's memories haunt him every day.

Johnny, told me his memories as we sat in a Maranatha camp in Beira, Mozambique. Two years before, Johnny's father hitched up their two oxen to their ancient wooden-wheeled cart, loaded the family into it, and started driving—all without saying a word. The oddest part of the journey was that his father hadn't loaded anything into the cart to sell in the market. Just the kids.

Though Johnny's parents were often silent, today they were especially so. The only sounds were the steady clump of the plodding oxen, the whispers and groans of the old, half-rotten cart, and the metallic clicks made as rocks squirmed under the weight of the iron rims. The road was dusty, and the day smelled dry.

The drive to town took a very long two hours. Distances in Africa are measured in time, not in miles or kilometers. No one in the village had ever owned a speedometer or even a watch. Time was measured by looking at the shadows that the sun cast on the ground.

Johnny was alert as they drove through the streets, his bright eyes scanning the surroundings, noticing things he had never seen before. Then his father stopped the oxen.

"Johnny," his father said, "our family doesn't have enough to feed all of us anymore. You are eight years old, and you are now on your own."

Eight-year-old Johnny stood on the curb and watched until the oxcart that he had played on as a child, rolled slowly off into the distance. His family was gone.

Johnny went back to one of the busier parts of town and became adept at living on the sidewalk. He swept it with great vigor every morning to let everyone know that he belonged there, that this was his place in town. Each day he

Ten-year-old Johnny, on his own since he was eight, was
badly injured by an oxcart when he was sleeping.

would go through the trash pile about a block down the street, sometimes finding spoiled fruit or maybe even a moldy goat hide that offered a piece of fat.

Daytime was easy. It was the nights that were long. One night as Johnny lay sleeping near the street, an oxcart driver missed his turn, lurched up onto Johnny's sidewalk, and crushed both of his feet. One of the shopkeepers decided to help Johnny out and set a cardboard refrigerator box out in the alley. This box became Johnny's new home. It wasn't much, but it was *his*.

Johnny's benefactor sold produce, and Johnny began to do anything and everything he could for his new friend, polishing each tomato as if it were made of precious metal, sweeping the floors, and greeting the customers.

Johnny's feet were an ever-worsening problem. They had become horribly infected from the open wounds made by the oxcart. It really hurt to walk, they smelled terrible, and Johnny was scared. That was when God sent two angels into Johnny's life—or rather "his" market.

Rachelle and Jen were two American college girls who had felt God's call to go on an adventure. Each had committed six months to doing whatever they could to help out the hundreds of Maranatha volunteers who were traveling to Mozambique. On this day, they were not out shopping for little boys to adopt, but for beans, tomatoes, cucumbers, and onions.

They gathered their groceries, but their conversation wasn't about the groceries. Rachelle and Jen were softly discussing what they could do for the little boy with infected feet. They couldn't just leave him, so they said a prayer, asking God what He would like them to do for Johnny.

God's answer was obvious. So they loaded Johnny up with their beans, tomatoes, cucumbers, and onions, and took him to a Maranatha rural medical clinic that was set up on the edge of town. The Maranatha doctors took one look and realized that the Maranatha outpost clinic wasn't set up for anything like this and Johnny needed to go to a hospital. But hospitals cost money, and money was something Johnny didn't have.

"That's OK," said the angels. The volunteers collected the needed money and Johnny's angels took him to the hospital.

The hospital doctors didn't have the means to treat Johnny either. All they could do was offer to amputate both feet. Not knowing what to do next, Rachelle and Jen brought Johnny to our Maranatha tent camp.

Dr. George Hill was our group leader on that trip, and he was at the tent village when Johnny arrived. George is an old navy doctor who has been around the world so many times he's lost count. "Not even battle wounds are this bad," George said after looking at Johnny's feet.

Johnny's feet had become so infected that the skin had sloughed off, leaving an ugly mass of muscle and tendons. His condition could have been caused by a flesh-eating bacteria; no one knew one way or the other.

Dr. George called the volunteers into action. Two young men helped Johnny take his first shower ever—the first time Johnny had bathed in a very long time. His blue jeans were so filthy that the boys had to cut them off to get them past his feet. Then Dr. George and his team began tending to Johnny's feet. Less than an hour later, our camp was filled with laughter, Johnny's laughter as he crawled around on the ground with giant white bandages covering both feet.

Then the angels recruited new help. Ronnie Kedas is a country director for Maranatha and a much-loved friend. He is also one very resourceful man. Before night had fallen, Ron had located a lady who would let Johnny set up a cot in her washroom. Her house wasn't much, and she already had mouths to feed, but she saw the need and agreed to take Johnny into her family.

Once again, the volunteers banded together to provide clothing, shoes, and money for Johnny and his new caregiver. During the next two weeks that the volunteers were in Mozambique, we had to buy four pairs of shoes for Johnny. No, he wasn't wearing them out, he was giving them away to other kids whom he thought needed them more than he did.

Johnny had already learned what so many Maranatha volunteers have discovered: nothing feels better than giving!

Several months later, Ronnie Kedas was making a trip that took him through Beira, so he stopped to check on Johnny. He found him happy in his new family and attending the school we built near the city.

We think angels come in many forms!

CHAPTER 39

Between a Rock and a School Campus

"Problems are only opportunities in work clothes."

—Henry J. Kaiser

I love a good challenge, especially if it is in Africa. We had just about completed the Manja school project in Malawi when Karen called from the Maranatha office and asked if we would be willing to stay in Africa a few more days and supervise the construction of a school in Bulawayo, Zimbabwe.

One thing I dislike about doing these mission trips is that the two weeks of building goes by much too quickly. Before you know it, we're back at the airport without having had the time to really see and experience the country and its people. When we return to the same place several times, we're able to dig deeper. It's like peeling an onion—sometimes you discover that the inside is sweeter than the outside.

Zimbabwe has a magical draw for us, an almost audible calling that we have felt from few other countries. I think part of it comes from the hardships the people have endured—from drought and famine, to political genocide and misdeeds. My observation is that the people are gentler, kinder, and softer in countries where there has been tremendous hardship. They are like well-worn pieces of fine cloth.

People here truly appreciate that they still exist, that they're alive, that they have families, and that they live in one of the most beautiful places on earth. Despite nearly impossible challenges, they haven't given up; they have endured and are eager to share what they have and to make new friends. During our many trips in Zimbabwe, I have discovered powerful life lessons, especially from the Bushmen, real men and women who value people over money, relationships over stuff.

There are many reasons to love Zimbabwe. There are also many opportunities to be challenged.

Dina and I flew to Livingstone, Zambia, crammed ourselves into Garwin Mc-Neilus's trusty Prado SUV with four helpers, tents, tools, clothes, and everything we thought we might need to stay at our destination for five days. Bulawayo was only five and a half hours away, but the only gas station between where we were and there was in the middle of nowhere, and often it had no gas. On this trip, the station had enough to fill our tank. Small victories make for happy trips!

We arrived at our destination without incident, but discovered that the steel for the new school building was still being held up in customs.

Plan A was for the container with the steel to have been delivered directly to the school building site. Unfortunately, the container was sitting ten miles away in a huge customs holding pen. It seems that an official seal on one of the customs documents wasn't raised quite enough. We didn't see that container while we were in Bulawayo, so the materials had to be borrowed from another site.

Plan B included a Mr. Beze, who had assured the local leaders that he had a truck lined up and that he would drive to Solusi Adventist University, pick up the steel that was left over from a previous building project, and bring it to us. But Mr. Beze wasn't answering his phone, so we drove around town till we found him! It took a bit of green persuasion, but he finally agreed to drive his small pickup truck to Solusi with us and bring back a load of steel. We cheered, believing that we would be able to start building on Sunday.

We drove to Solusi Friday afternoon, loaded Mr. Beze's pickup and Garwin's Prado with as much weight as we felt they might safely haul, and bounced slowly back to Bulawayo. We were now on Plan C.

Friday was almost gone when we arrived in Barbour Fields, a suburb of Bulawayo. The following day was the Saturday, which God meant to give us time to recharge our spiritual batteries. We headed for Matopos National Park bright and early, eager to see its fascinating collection of humongous granite boulders stacked on top of each other. It looked like a monstrous giant had set up a vast stone city and then walked off to find another playground.

Just before reaching the park, we made three new "friends"—the hard way. With machine guns in hand, the three policemen waved us over and demanded one hundred and fifty U.S. dollars for driving too fast on a section of road they were patrolling. I told them that all I had with me was fifty dollars, and that if they needed more, they would have to take me to jail. That was not an easy prospect for them because they didn't have a vehicle at their disposal. After a bit of banter and discussion, we finally agreed on fifty dollars and a handful of sweets, a fine that one of my good Zimbabwean friends told me was still five times too high. "Next time, just give them ten dollars and drive off," was his advice.

Matopos Park is an amazing place. Rocks the size of three-bedroom houses stand precariously balanced on much smaller pillars. Every bend of the road offers new views of cathedrals, castles, bears, and more. There's even a stone that looks like U.S. President Richard Nixon.

Rhodesia's favorite son and premier Cecil Rhodes loved this place so much that he asked to be buried on a hillside strewn with red boulders the size of Big

Ben. (In the colonial days, Zimbabwe was known as Rhodesia.) The British government had appointed Rhodes to be the premier of Rhodesia. When he died, in 1902, he was the first white man to be buried with the royal Matabele salute, Bayete. The Rhodes government donated many large tracts of land to Christian missionary groups, encouraging them to build schools for the Matabele and Zulu people. Rhodes was also the first foreigner to discover diamonds in this part of Africa.

I had already taken photos of rocks, rocks, and more rocks, and was ready to find the storied Matopos petroglyphs. We followed the map and found nothing. Finally, after considerable hiking through some really rough terrain looking for ancient paintings I couldn't find, I stumbled onto a Bushman flat in the middle of nowhere. "Why are you lost out here?" he asked.

When I told him I was looking for the petroglyphs—paintings on the rocks— his eyes lit up as if he was savoring a memory of the past. "In my village," he said, "there are rock paintings that are outside of the park and are never visited. They are completely unprotected."

He had my undivided attention. The words "Can you take me there?" were out of my mouth before I had time to think.

"I can," he replied, "but it's a long drive and a long hike from here."

Of course, I didn't consider that to be a problem, so we climbed into our four-wheel-drive and started down the road.

That road got narrower and rougher, deteriorating from a half-decent dirt road to an impassible goat trail. Finally, we arrived at the Bushman's tiny village, and the four-wheel-drive could go no farther. One by one the children who were playing outside disappeared, returning a few minutes later with some rags on their backs. The village was remote enough that people wore clothes only when company came.

Dina and I looked at each other. I was concerned about leaving her all alone in a strange village, but our Bushman guide assured us that she would be fine. So I waved goodbye and struck out after my guide, carrying enough camera gear with me to shoot a wedding.

The afternoon was sticky hot, and my guide stepped along quickly. He was such a little guy that I felt I couldn't ask him to help me with my gear, so I struggled to keep up.

We climbed for well over an hour, through scratchy brambles and narrow crevices on a trail that it was obvious no one had used since forever. After making several wrong turns, my Bushman friend confessed that it had been more than ten years since he had visited the petroglyphs on the mountain.

As we trekked farther and farther from civilization, it slowly dawned on me that this was a good place to make somebody vanish forever! The cameras in my backpack were worth more than my guide could earn in a lifetime, and I began to wonder if he was really a friend.

Suddenly, he stopped and pointed to a large stone overhang. Running across it from one side to another were detailed painted stories that I could have reached out and touched. It was a sacred place where ancient artists had filled a wall with scenes of hunters chasing their prey, a finely etched zoo of various animals. The light was fading, but opportunity was calling. We stayed beneath the overhang for forty-five minutes, during which I shot hundreds of pictures. Then we were once again scratching our legs on the brambles as we followed the setting sun to the village.

The red hues of the ancient ink were still vivid on the stone walls of the Matopos Cliffs.

My guide took a different trail down the mountain; one that took us past the ruins of a small village. Now, only remnants of the mud walls of a few dwellings remained. We had been gone more than four hours, so rather than photograph the village, we dashed on down the hill till our four-wheeler came into sight.

I was relieved to see Dina and the vehicle, and Dina was even more relieved to see me. Her imagination had been running wild during those four hours. She'd been imagining that I would never come back—that the Bushman had taken me into the desolate, empty wilderness to rob and kill me. She had even imagined me bitten by a flashy, poisonous green mamba! And the longer her wait became, the wilder her imagination ran.

The kids in the village, however, were absolutely intrigued. They had never seen a blue-eyed, blond human being in their lives. Every kid in the village was there, wanting to touch the woman with the pale skin. And once I was back, Dina was able to enjoy the kids in turn. Then it became hard to tell who found the other more entertaining—the kids or Dina, who was continually asking if we could bring one home.

The homemade toys these kids had were cool. They crafted their pistols from the spokes of an old bicycle wheel. Their little guns were so powerful that they could shoot a hollow reed more than forty feet. Their spinning tops were made of wood, and they braided horsehair ropes with which to spin them. Their slings were impressive too; they could take down small game. Both Dina and I came away amazed at the ingenuity we found in this really primitive place.

The sun was setting as we headed back to the park and the road to our room. We drove in silence for quite a while as the road took us beneath the hanging boulders of Matopos. Once again, my heart was moved by the integrity and kindness of my Bushman friend. My world was far from his. He had never gone to school, would never visit a big city, and would never drive a car. I had felt safe in his care, and he hadn't let me down. I had made a new friend.

Morning came early. By a quarter to five we had left our room and headed back to Solusi Adventist University, the only other place in all of Zimbabwe where we had any extra materials we could use on the steel school building we were assembling. As is usually the case in Africa, the sun put on a spectacular show as it rose, and thousands of locals were walking on the sides of the road, taking advantage of the coolness of the morning to travel from home to work in the city. It takes an hour to drive from Bulawayo to Solusi, and we were glad we had left early because once again Mr. Beze had left us high and dry. We decided we were going to have to mount a full-scale search for a truck.

Several hours later, we finally located a truck we could use. It was an ancient farm truck, with no brakes, stringy tires, broken headlights, and an engine that had emphysema. We thanked God for the truck, and asked Him to keep it alive as we drove to Bulawayo and back. Then we loaded it and Garwin's Prado with hundreds of pieces of steel and began the arduous return to town.

Hauling slippery pieces of steel sixteen feet long atop a Prado SUV is a delicate task. Tap the gas or the brakes too hard, and it's reloading time!

I'm the guy who loves challenges, especially if they are in exotic places. On this trip, God certainly gave me enough to lock in my memory forever!

One of the hardest challenges was charging the batteries in our American-made cordless drills. Zimbabwe has a British heritage, so it is a 220-volt nation. But DeWalt tools come from America, so they require 110-volt power. We had brought a simple converter along, and it should have done the trick, but our drills simply refused to charge while on the converter. We spent a good share of that workday trying to charge our American-made batteries—and failing.

Part of the crew got a good workout cutting the steel to match the building needs. Usually we are able to do this with a power saw, but the only working saw we had was a very primitive hacksaw. At about every third push or pull, the hacksaw blade tried to jump out of the frame.

After losing most of the day, we went to the Adventist conference office in Bulawayo, where we were warmly received and offered the use of a 220-volt generator and several corded tools. Now that we had the tools and the steel, we could lay out the school campus. We worked until it was too dark to see, arriving back in our hotel room after 10:00 P.M.

The local church members were highly supportive and did whatever they could to help us. The Dorcas women did our cooking and cleaned up the rest of the property. The men helped us move and raise the steel.

Another challenge we faced on that trip was to move a one-day church that had been built a couple of years before. Since then, the leaders had decided that the place where the church stood was the perfect location for a school. Unfortunately, that meant the church had to be moved. We decided to try to move the building completely intact—without disassembling it.

After preparing the stakes on the new site, which was about half a block away, I had the crew remove all screws holding the church to its foundation except one on each side. Since there was a small breeze, we put more people on the windy side, to counter the additional force the wind brought to that side. When the crew removed the last screws, the entire weight of the church structure was being held by thirty-six church members. Then, lifting and grunting and pointing, we carried the one-day church to its new location.

As you can guess, the involvement of the church members was the highlight of this project. They came early and stayed as late as we did every night, which was until it was too dark to see. Then they would find their way back to their homes, which had no electricity, and go to bed by candlelight.

The total time it took to build the combination church and auditorium on the campus of the new school? About two full days. The challenge was rounding up the components and proper tools. That's kind of normal—in life, experience teaches that preparation is always the key. Without it, we can never execute properly.

CHAPTER 40

Nuts From God

"Impossibilities vanish when a man and his God confront a mountain."

—Robert Schuller

The foundations were in, and the volunteers were on their way. More than a thousand children in Victoria Falls, Zimbabwe, would soon be able to go to school.

All the steel for the new school buildings had been shipped from the one-day school manufacturing facility in Dodge Center, Minnesota. The steel comes to that plant in giant rolls that weigh more than ten tons each, one per flatbed truck. The trucks back up to one of the doors on the receiving dock of the plant, and cranes lift the roll from the truck and move it—very carefully—into the processing line for flattening, cutting, bending, and drilling the twenty-seven different pieces required to make a one-day school. A few days later, another flatbed pulls out of the other end of the manufacturing facility carrying a carefully packed container marked for delivery to a school site somewhere in the world. The container travels by land from Minnesota to Baltimore, Maryland, and then by sea to an entry port in Africa, India, Central America, the South Pacific, or to an island in the Caribbean.

The containers carrying the steel and assembly tools for the new Victoria Falls school landed in Durban, South Africa. Customs officials there opened the containers and checked the written list of contents against the detailed list painted inside the door of each container. They crawled into the container and lifted a few pieces of steel just to be sure that nothing extra was hidden inside, and then they slammed the container doors shut and locked. Then another crane lifted each container onto a flatbed truck, and the drivers were directed north through South Africa, past the kingdom of Swaziland, and through most of Zimbabwe, to the town of Victoria Falls.

Thousands of miles from Minnesota, a team from Maranatha Volunteers

International directed the drivers to the new school site in a suburb overflowing with eager school-age children. There aren't enough schools for all the kids in Victoria Falls, and though they might be able to go to school through third grade, planning for anything beyond that was pure folly. Until now.

The list of the container's contents painted in black on the inside of the right-side door is a list of absolutely everything that has been packed in the container, and it's a very long list. Often the container carries the power tools, generators, nuts, bolts, and window material along with the necessary steel. Every item is listed.

Mkhosana, the Victoria Falls school, is a very large project. That means five trucks dropped five containers at the site where the new school would stand. The Maranatha workers immediately began emptying the steel boxes, and, as if an especially awesome Christmas morning were approaching, they stacked everything under the mango trees. That way the pieces would be where volunteers could get to them quickly as they assembled the buildings.

Everything was there—except for one thousand steel nuts.

These buildings have plexi-glass windows in steel frames. Each window is fastened to the wall with four bolts, each of which is supposed to have two nuts to hold it in place. It's a simple design; one that inexperienced volunteers can assemble in places where building materials aren't readily available—places like the African bush. The window materials were all there in the container—steel, plexi-glass, and five hundred bolts.

But no nuts. They were still in Minnesota!

No problem. Just go down to Home Depot and buy new nuts, right?

Wrong.

There's no Home Depot in Victoria Falls. There's no Lowe's. There's no ACE or any other hardware store, except for a small (very small) building on a back street. You might be able to find a hammer or two there, but certainly no nuts.

So the building construction leaders checked every other nearby town.

No nuts.

That's when one of the leaders turned to Moses, a tall Zimbabwean man who had been hired to work with the volunteers, and asked him to help.

"You speak the Ndebele language, so I am going to ask you to help us fix the window problem. Please go down to the hardware man in Victoria Falls and buy one thousand nuts that fit this bolt."

The two men both knew the problem, so they prayed together before Moses set off on his impossible errand.

The bolt hung heavy in Moses' pocket as he walked into the small store. "Please, may I speak to the oldest man here?" Moses asked.

An ancient African shuffled to the dusty counter and said, "How may I help you?"

"I am working for the Maranatha company that is building the new school out toward the airport—you know, the big Adventist one where we've had to chase the elephants away."

"Yes, I know of the school," the man answered. "I don't think they can get the school built in two weeks like they say."

"It's going to be a challenge, but I think it can be done," Moses responded. "But we have a problem."

Moses reached deep into his pocket, pulled out the shiny, new steel bolt, and continued. "To hold the windows in the school walls, we need one thousand nuts that fit this bolt. They were supposed to be in one of the containers of supplies, but somehow they were left out. Could we buy what we need from you?"

Moses handed the bolt to the old man, who looked at it closely and then handed it to one of the younger men in his store. "Americans are so crazy," the man said. "Everyone else uses the metric system, but the Americans have to be different and stick with their old system, so metric nuts won't fit on the bolts they use. This is one of those American bolts. I haven't even seen anything that uses that system for more than fifty years. So, no, I can't sell you any nuts for your bolts. And I don't have any metric bolts and nuts that would do the job. Sorry."

That started a hurricane of conversation. Everyone at the counter wanted to talk about the nuts and the bolts, standard versus metric, Americans versus the British, and whether the Adventists were going to be able to finish the new school.

"Sir," Moses interrupted, "I know all of this is true, but would you please do a very big favor for me? Please go into your storage room and see if just maybe you have one thousand standard nuts that would fit this bolt. Please!"

The request brought raucous laughter—but also the condescending agreement of the store owner. "I'll go look," he said. Then he took the bolt and walked toward the back of the store.

Many minutes later, the man walked back to the counter, looked Moses directly in the eye, and said, "I have a story to tell you. Sixty years ago, a white Rhodesian farmer came to this store and asked us to order for him one thousand number twelve bolts, standard size—exactly like the bolt you gave me. We agreed, and I sent a letter to an American supplier. The supplier agreed, but he required that we purchase bolts *and* nuts. The farmer said that was OK, so we placed the order.

"When the box came, I contacted the farmer, and he came to town and told me he wanted only the bolts! He paid me and left me with the boxes of one thousand nuts."

Everyone crowded around as the man placed the boxes on the counter, took two nuts, and screwed them onto the bolt Moses had brought.

"I've had these on a shelf in the back room for nearly sixty years. I haven't thought about them for years. I haven't noticed them. They've just collected dust—until today."

Moses paid for the nuts and carried them back to the Maranatha project manager. "One thousand standard nuts, sir," he said with a smile.

One of the volunteers was standing nearby and heard the story. "Imagine how much work the angels from Heavenly Supply had to do to make sure we had one thousand standard nuts in Victoria Falls today!" he said.

That started a new hurricane of conversation, and a season of prayers of thanksgiving.

"Imagine," one volunteer said, "the angels knew the bolts would be missing, so sixty years ago they convinced a farmer he needed one thousand standard bolts, size twelve. Bolts only. No nuts."

"Even more," another added, "they then had to get an American hardware supplier to sell only bolts *with* nuts!"

"And a farmer to agree to pay for both."

"And then to decide to leave the nuts here in this store—for us!"

"I wonder how the angels kept the store owner and employees from seeing the boxes on that shelf?"

"And then, today, they swept away the cobwebs, blew away the dust, and pointed the store owner right at them."

The room filled with silence as everyone thought about nuts and bolts and angels.

"If God had angels watch over these nuts for sixty years," someone said, "I wonder what He's already done to take care of the stuff that's worrying me today!"

TOMORROW

CHAPTER 41

Volunteers Need Love Too

*"Understand how beautifully God has added one more day to your life—
not because you need it, but because someone else needs you."*

—Unknown

The more I go on Maranatha projects, the more I realize that I go in order to be with the volunteers rather than to build the buildings. My heart is now focused on effecting change in the lives of the volunteers—on getting them to think differently about themselves and the world in the five or six workdays I have with them.

I remember well the days when I milked cows at Platte Valley Academy. I told my boss that I knew how to milk cows because back at home I had milked two cows by hand every day. He smiled and pointed me down the hall to the 127 cows that needed to be milked. For weeks I felt like my life was in a big whirl, as if someone had thrown me into a huge dairy-barn blender and turned it up to Super High! Stuff was flying all over the place, including me. I was kicked down into the gutter more than once. I carried pails of milk that weighed more than I did. I prayed for each morning to end. My mornings were a slow-motion nightmare from which I couldn't wake up.

We don't want the volunteers who come to work on our projects to ever have that feeling. Some arrive with this really cool new tool belt that they have never used, and they're nervous. I hand them a screw gun and remind them to be sure it's in forward rather than reverse, and they look at me like a goat looks at a watch. They have no idea what I am talking about. They had no idea there were gears on a screw gun! There are so many things on a project that have never been part of their world.

At Platte Valley, my boss took me down to the milking line, introduced me to his cows, showed me how to use the mechanical milking machines, and stayed to guide me through the process. That's what I try to do on each project. We start with quick, basic, 101-level classes on screw guns, job safety, water drinking (dehydration), block laying, and personal hygiene.

But there are things even more important than tape measures and screw guns.

It's easy for volunteers to get a sense of how "poor and needy the people are down here." It's much more difficult to get a sense of "how blessed I am to have what I have."

I want each volunteer to realize how blessed he or she is, how fortunate we are to have grown up where we did, and how much God is already involved—and how eager He is to become more involved—in their lives. We want these realizations to change every bit of how we live. As one teenage Pathways volunteer told me, "I'll never shop the same again!"

If we can't change them some in the time we have them, I doubt they'll ever change. If we don't succeed, the next time they're exposed to real needs in the lives of people who are poor, hungry, sick, and hurting, maybe it's because they have been hardened and may not even notice the need.

One of the lessons I've learned is that volunteers tend to become tired after a few days on the job, so if we push a little more up front at the beginning of the project, I don't have to flog them when they start running out of gas.

It's OK to become tired after six days of working hard in the full sun when the temperature is over 100 degrees and the humidity is above 90 percent, but we're still going to get the job done! I've mapped the project schedule and even added a rain day. We're OK!

It's important that I check the project schedule several times each day. Sometimes leaders have to steer the boat away from the rocks and back into the channel again. If I've done my job well, I'm the only one who has to worry about the schedule.

Here's a very simple little strategy for getting into the hearts and minds of the volunteers in six days. It isn't a big deal—you just walk around and see what's going on. That makes your job as the leader one that offers the most fun.

The dynamics of every group and every project are different, but the little six-step strategy that follows works every time.

1. Break the comfort zone. Get the volunteers out of their comfort zones. Being away from home, away from their electronic assistants, and away from their daily routines puts them just a little off kilter and makes them more open to the Holy Spirit.

2. Develop a new comfort zone. One of my goals on the worksite is to help each volunteer develop a new comfort zone. I help them discover where they would be most comfortable working and then help them take ownership of that task. If they're afraid of ladders, I give them a ground-level job. If they hate getting dirty, I assign them to something near—but not in the middle of—dirt. I treat them as I think I would like to be treated.

There are all kinds of jobs for all kinds of volunteers. My job is to help connect each one with the duties that will give him or her the most success. Their comfort zones don't need to be large. This serves most as a base for the third and fourth parts of my strategy.

3. Affirm individually. Everyone wants to do a good job, so I assign each volunteer carefully and then work with each one individually for a few minutes, helping each person learn to do the job I've given them the right way. Then I get out of the way to go and help others. After thirty or forty minutes, I circle back around to check on their work and to affirm them personally, to affirm the job they've done, and to suggest possible improvements.

Affirmation is the key. I often have to make several return trips before they begin to feel OK and successful. Most people are not at home on a construction job. They're in a new environment and are unsure of what the end product should look like. They are lawyers, schoolteachers, accountants, gravediggers, and more. The common thread is that they've never done construction.

Amazingly, some volunteers can be full of doubts—uncertainties that have been planted and watered by bosses, family members, and friends. Those small words of criticism, often spoken without thought, are incredibly destructive. Why not turn the tables and affirm them instead? And do it in such a way that others can hear them being affirmed. When the people they're working with hear me say, "You can do it," they hear, "*We* can do it."

I affirm the hats they wear, the slogans on their shirts, their drinking lots of water, the careful cleaning of the bricks—anything I can! Affirm, affirm, affirm. One "Cool hat!" breaks through years of "Why are you wearing that ugly dress again?"

One reason I affirm in such a way that others can hear is to set the tone on the worksite. People are reassured when they know that they are part of a successful team. My goals for the volunteers include a safe working environment—a place where everyone is valued. Since most folks don't live or work in a place like that, I work hard to create a special new world on this job—a world where people are nurtured, where they can explore and challenge without retribution.

I love affirming people because affirmation changes everything!

4. Challenge for improvement. Circulating among my team provides numerous opportunities for me to demonstrate simpler and better ways to do the jobs. Everyone wants to do their best, so they're usually receptive to counsel; especially since most of them are doing something they haven't done for a long time or maybe have never done. I keep myself always receptive to counsel because there are many ways to skin a cat, and one of the volunteers may know the best way to get something done.

When you're challenging someone to improve, simple demonstrations work well, especially if they're accompanied by affirmation. "You can do it!"

Sometimes all they need is for me to pat them on the back or to use a tone of voice that lets them know I care. That's good mental and emotional nourishment, and it encourages people whose bodies are asking them why they suddenly have to work so hard! Most people would gladly take a cut in their pay in exchange for being acknowledged as personally valuable.

If it's obvious that someone has been assigned to a job that doesn't fit his or her gifts, I help them discover and find what fits better and begin helping them get comfortable in their new role. People often surprise me by what they're able to do, and usually it's a surprise that exceeds their own expectations.

As I look at the project and walk around and connect with every person on it, I'm continually assessing whether each person is happy at what he or she is doing and if they're doing a good job of what they're doing. If they're happy but are doing a bad job, we can change the job and make them even happier!

I circulate a lot—all day, every day. I circulate when we're on the job and when we're sitting around the meal tables at our camp. Every minute is a diamond waiting to be cut, so I keep circulating till we get off the plane at home. And sometimes I continue to do it for years, on Facebook and on the phone.

5. Love the locals. I love the Maranatha mission statement: "We build people while building urgently needed buildings." That statement gives me permission to get the construction done while focusing on the real reason the volunteers have come—to effect change in their lives.

Yes, I know they said they came to change others, but in the end it will be the volunteers themselves who will change the most. I still experience this on every trip. It's just one of the many things that continues to draw me back.

Rub shoulders with the culture. Some days it's OK to eat worms or *shima* with *carpenta* (corn mush with small, sun-dried fish). Experience how this part of the world lives. Learn about the choices they have to make each day—often without many other options.

God created all of us equal. The single biggest difference between the locals and us volunteers is where we were born. Aside from that, we're just the same.

We frequently have the privilege of working alongside the locals. Teach them a skill. Empower them so they can feed their families long after you've gone home. Share your knowledge. Brighten their horizons. Build a bridge of friendship.

And let them know they are loved. The desire to be loved lies deep in the core of each of us, no matter what part of the world we grew up in. Convey the message that we are all brothers and sisters.

6. Love your people. How many of us in this old world could use a bit more love? Not just words rolling off the tongue, but genuine caring from another human being. It's amazing how much better we feel when we know we are accepted, appreciated, and valued.

Discover that it's actually fun to love those who are not so loveable. It's surprising how the dynamics can change when people know you really care. Often, those with the most formidable facades are the ones who need love the most. Deep down, they want to give the love back too, and they will if you show them love first.

Take the time to let others know you care, and you will feel the love coming right back. That is one of the really unique things about love; it is always a two-way street. What you send out returns.

I love stories. Stories about our previous mission trips. Stories I've heard from old missionaries or gleaned from a distant village. Stories about the fellow selling plastic bottles down the road. Stories about the teachers who will be teaching in the school we're building. Stories I wish someone had shared with me on my first trip.

I enjoy worships. Worships that feature great promises like those found in Jeremiah 29, one of the most meaningful chapters I've found in Scripture. I want each worship to be full of praise and prayers, to be times of holy praise that lead us back to God and the joy of being loved by Him.

It is fun to introduce locals to the volunteers. Sometimes that means introducing people who are full-time local Maranatha employees like Elijah and Richard and Marta to the volunteers. Often the friend I'm introducing is a woodcarver I met in the market, or an artist who's using one of my photos to paint a masterpiece. Sometimes we introduce individual volunteers to a local person I "just know" they'll love. So many of the locals have amazing stories of survival and personal hardship that it's often difficult to choose which ones to bring to our camp for storytime.

My goal is for each volunteer to sense the real needs of the people we've come to serve and then to adopt the people and the place. That's what Jesus would do!

CHAPTER 42

My Bucket List

Follow your heart. It will take you to places you have never been before.

What's on my bucket list? (You know, the list of things I want to do before I die.) It seems to be getting shorter as I grow older. There are still a few things on the list:

→ *Fly in a jet fighter*
  I'd love to be in the pilot's seat of a jet fighter going about 650 knots, look up through the canopy, and then push the throttles open, pull the nose straight up, and go to Mach 2.5. That would be a rush.

→ *Make a pass in a top fuel car*
  Eight thousand horsepower plastering me to the seat; hitting 325 miles per hour in less than four seconds. OK, so I used to be an adrenaline junkie. I think my angel is too.

At one time these first two were both very high on my list. I'll never get to do them, but bucket lists are about dreams, aren't they?

→ *Write a book*
  (This one has been on the list since I was twelve.) Maybe I'd write about some of the interesting twists and turns we have experienced in our wanderings around the world. I hope it would be something that people want to read and that it would contain thoughts that would make their lives better and maybe include some real-life experiences showing God at work, providing evidence that we are not alone.

→ *Live to see Jesus return*
THIS is my daily prayer. When I was a child, it seemed to me that the world was in turmoil. Now we live our whole lives knowing that at any moment someone might press the wrong button. Even if God chooses not to heal me of cancer, this item is still very possible in my opinion. The thought also gives me great hope and courage.

→ *Travel to Antarctica, Australia, Pakistan, and/or the South Seas*
I'm pretty sure I could spend a month in a canoe in the South Seas—two months if I had my cameras. There are so many places we haven't explored yet. Instead of feeling that I'm well traveled, I feel like a tiny speck in a massive universe. Especially in India.

→ *Take as many friends and family with me as I can*
I want to take them not just on the travels through life but to Heaven. What better place to enjoy our friends and loved ones than in an environment that is completely nurturing and pain and stress free. A place where we at last can have all the quality time we want to spend together. I anticipate a grand reunion of maximum proportions.

I don't think there's as much on my bucket list as there used to be. I think bucket lists change as we change—as our values and interests shift with the realities of life. When I was young, I wanted to have a fast car, a hot wife, and live happily ever after. I've had hot cars, and I love my hot wife, but for me, "happily ever after" no longer includes the smell of burning rubber. My values have changed, and so have the things I would most like to be and do. Right now, living past sixty is pretty important to me.

The act that gives me the most confidence during my days and nights is prayer. When is a good time to pray? I have found that I can pray in the shower, while driving down the road, when I wake up, when I go to bed, and just about anytime in between. Prayer doesn't have to be formal; you're talking to a friend. Be direct; say what's on your mind. The God we serve is so amazing that despite the difference between who He is and who we are, He's waiting to hear from us—He *delights* in hearing from us! For us to admit to God that we need His presence in our lives is the key to an amazing relationship with Him.

The other thing that God loves to hear is praise. Praise for life, for health, and for all of the other blessings that He shares with us. It's OK to whisper to Him our needs and desires. Make praise a major part of your prayer time. It's amazing how our gratitude increases when we review all that we have to be thankful for. Rejoice in hope because hope makes all the difference. Let your ministry exude hope. Let hope make a difference in your life. Let your hope make a difference in someone else's life.

Continue to praise God for the opportunities and possibilities He puts in our lives. And never, never, ever give up.

I'll say it again. Undoubtedly, prayer is one of the most powerful things in my life. Not only have I obtained power in answer to my prayers, but I've also found that I gain power from being prayed for and from knowing that I am being prayed for. More than three years have passed since the doctors told me that I wouldn't be here anymore, and yet I continue to live. I absolutely have to credit my continued existence to the power of prayer.

I have also found it very affirming to pray for others and to let them know that I'm praying for them, that I care for them. The knowledge that someone is lifting them up in prayer assures them that they are not alone.

Prayer can most certainly change your circumstances. It opens doors that we cannot open. We have certainly seen this to be true many times over. When a door does open, have the courage to walk through it. No one will pick you up and carry you through that open door; you must take that step yourself.

There will be times of doubt, make no mistake about it. But these can be some of the best times to approach God and make yourself available to Him. Who knows what He has in store for you? I can assure you of one thing: His plans for your life are much more exciting than your own.

Here's a question worth pondering: What is the true purpose of your friendships? Is it bragging rights on your Facebook page? Are your "friends" merely rungs on your ladder to success—rungs that you step on in the process? I believe that every friendship has a purpose, and that purpose is to lift each other up, to encourage and help each other.

To be a friend, we have to accept people exactly as they are. We aren't in the business of changing people; only God can do that. Our task is to reflect His light in our lives. He does the rest.

Relationship is the term for our interactions with others. It can take years to build trust with someone, but that trust, that relationship can be destroyed in a second. And it can happen so many different ways. Sometimes you see it coming, and sometimes it's a complete surprise.

The relationships we've built have given us the privilege of walking with some amazing people. A few that come to mind are Basil, the Lion King, and Dr. Han. And what's true in the realm of this earth is true of our spiritual life as well. If we want to have a successful walk with Christ, we have to develop a relationship with Him.

Some of the best advice I have ever gotten is to "stay true to who you are." Another good piece of advice? Life is a two-way street. If all the flow is going one direction, an accident is bound to happen. Relationships are built on the trust and honesty of both parties.

Now I need to turn your attention to some really hard questions, ones designed to drag you out of your comfort zone. Have you ever thought about God's plans for your life? Each of us has been given a different task. What is your task?

What about the gifts that God has entrusted to you, how are you using them?

Are they benefiting only you, or are others being blessed by them also? If you were never born, how would the world be different? If you died today, what would the headlines be? What kind of mark have you left on this world?

Every day is an opportunity to make a difference, and what a difference we can make! We don't all have to travel around the world; that may not be what God has called you to do. Instead, the place where God wants you to reflect the light of Christ might be right across the street or at the place where you work. Don't try to be the light; be content to reflect His light.

Am I still flawed? Unfortunately, the answer is Yes. We all are; we're humans. None of us is perfect.

Can God use us despite our flaws? Of course He can and He does. In fact, He's been doing it for as long as this world has been in existence. God delights in using broken people to advance His gospel. God delights in using you and me.

I really enjoy living—being a part of life. I'm sure that statement is true for most of us. However, just because we're here now doesn't guarantee us even another minute of life. Every breath we take, every thought and heartbeat is just a part of God's gift to us. What we do with these gifts is our gift to Him. Strive to live an intentional life—one directed with purpose.

I have been both humbled and blessed while traveling the world. I love what someone has said—the statement about connecting the dots in the world, and the thought that the more dots we connect, the smaller the world becomes. I hope that Dina and I have an increased understanding of other cultures and continents other than our own, having made friends in many lands.

My hope is that this book will encourage you to seek and explore God's plan for your life. May you also be encouraged to continue to press on no matter what life's challenges might be, no matter how insurmountable the odds you face might seem. We don't always get to choose our path in life, but we do get to choose who walks with us.

God, thank You for extending my life and keeping death at bay until it's Your time to call me home. Until then, please give me grace to serve You wholeheartedly.

Greeting another spectacular day on the Indian Ocean.

Five in the morning in Xai-Xai, Mozambique. Dad, my brother Bruce (on the right), and I are watching another spectacular sunrise on the Indian Ocean.

A bird's-eye view of Havana, Cuba.

Rock formations in Matopos National Park, Zimbabwe.

The mighty Ucayali, headwaters to the Amazon, is the playground for these boys. Staying alive is the first thing they learn.

To crouch down and let these big cats walk past is a rush and a half! As they walked by, they leaned in and rubbed against me. Their heads were a foot above mine.